Three Good Things: An Appreciation Journal

Published by DARE Wellness

First edition; First printing

Illustrations and design

© Pip Cody 2016

www.darewellness.com

ISBN 978-1-326-68619-2

Three Good Things

This journal grew out of my wish to practise appreciating the good things in my life more.

The word "appreciation" in English actually has three meanings:

1. Recognition and enjoyment of the good qualities of someone or something
2. A full understanding of a situation
3. An increase in value

Research in the field of positive psychology has shown that taking the time to fully appreciate three good things in our life each day leads to greater wellbeing and happiness. Writing about things that have gone well encourages us to notice, savour, and remember the things that make our lives better.

As we enjoy these good things, understanding them fully, they become even more valuable to us.

If you're like me, you might struggle to actually do this practice consistently, despite your best intentions. That's where this journal comes in. I found that having a specific journal, and choosing a specific time and place to write in it, really helped me to establish the habit of appreciating on a daily basis. I hope it helps you too.

The facing pages feature quotes which may prompt you to think about appreciation in new ways. The designs on these pages can be coloured in, while you relax and contemplate the quote, or reflect on what you have written.

There might be times when writing about three good things feels too difficult. That's ok. On those occasions, I'd encourage you to just write about one good thing. From my experience, I'd say that fully appreciating just one good thing is more beneficial than doing a superficial job on three things... and infinitely better than not doing it at all.

Three Good Things

The practice:

Each day, write down three things that went well, and explain **why** they went well. Who contributed to those events? What made them possible?

They can be big things, or they can be relatively minor, it really doesn't matter.

First, give the event a title. For example, "I wrote 1000 words for my book", or "Lunch with my best friend".

Then, write about the event in as much detail as possible. What did you do? What did you think? What did you say? Were other people involved? What did they do? What did they say?

Reflect on how you felt – both at the time, and afterwards. How are you feeling about it now, as you reflect on it?

Finally, explain what caused this event to happen, or made it possible. Is it the result of actions you've taken? Who else has helped to make it possible? What other contributing factors are there?

Use any writing style you like, and don't get too hung up on spelling, grammar, or neat handwriting… no-one is going to be assessing you on this!

If other feelings come up, such as grief, or sadness, see if you can just make room for them. They belong here too. This practise is not about pretending that everything in life is wonderful. It's just a matter of remembering to notice and appreciate the things that are.

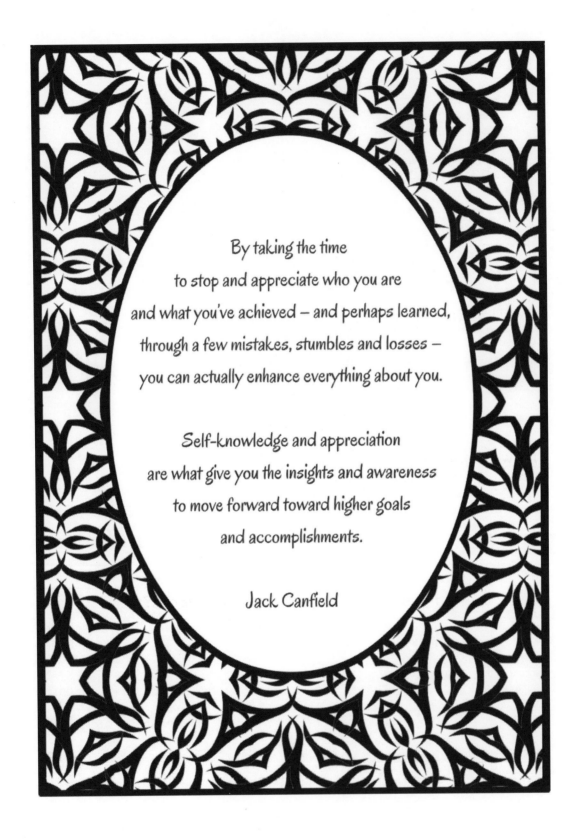

By taking the time
to stop and appreciate who you are
and what you've achieved – and perhaps learned,
through a few mistakes, stumbles and losses –
you can actually enhance everything about you.

Self-knowledge and appreciation
are what give you the insights and awareness
to move forward toward higher goals
and accomplishments.

Jack Canfield

Title:

What happened:

How I felt at the time:

How I felt later:

What caused this to happen in the way that it did?

Appreciation
is a wonderful thing:

It makes
what is excellent in others
belong to us as well.

Voltaire

Today's Date:_____

Title:

What happened:

How I felt at the time:

How I felt later:

What caused this to happen in the way that it did?

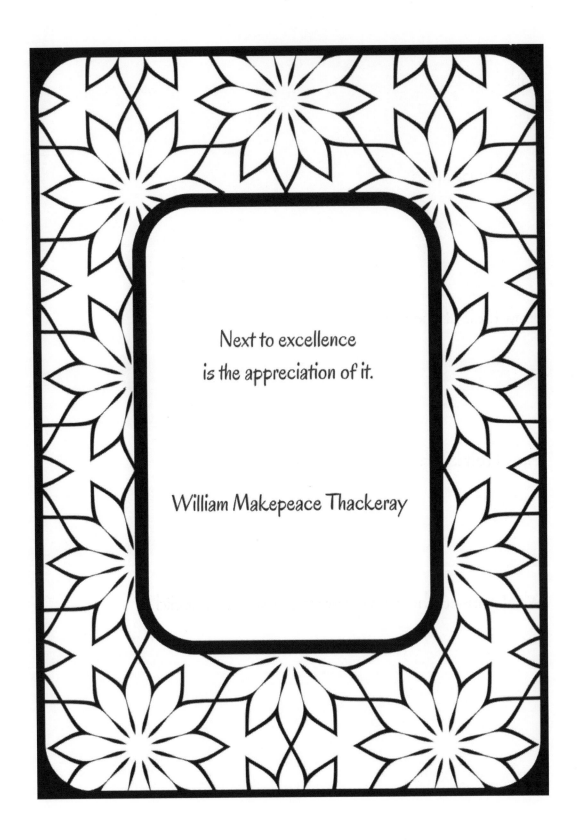

Next to excellence
is the appreciation of it.

William Makepeace Thackeray

Title:

What happened:

How I felt at the time:

How I felt later:

What caused this to happen in the way that it did?

The roots
of all goodness
lie in the soil of
appreciation for goodness.

Tenzin Gyatso
The 14th Dalai Lama

Today's Date:_____

Title:

What happened:

How I felt at the time:

How I felt later:

What caused this to happen in the way that it did?

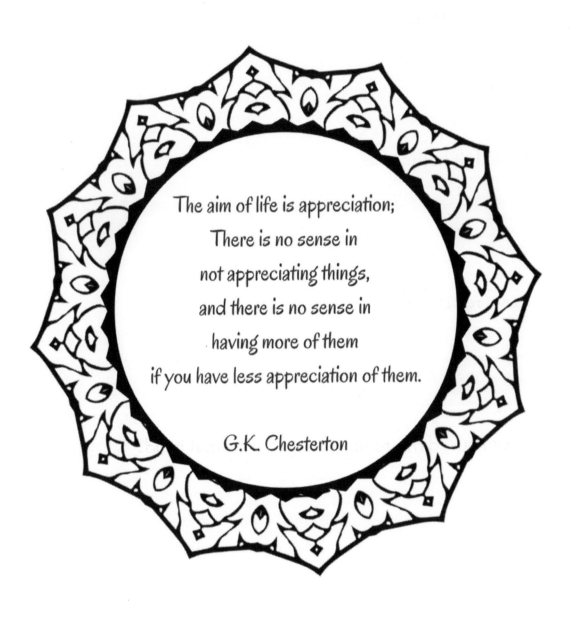

The aim of life is appreciation;
There is no sense in
not appreciating things,
and there is no sense in
having more of them
if you have less appreciation of them.

G.K. Chesterton

Title:

What happened:

How I felt at the time:

How I felt later:

What caused this to happen in the way that it did?

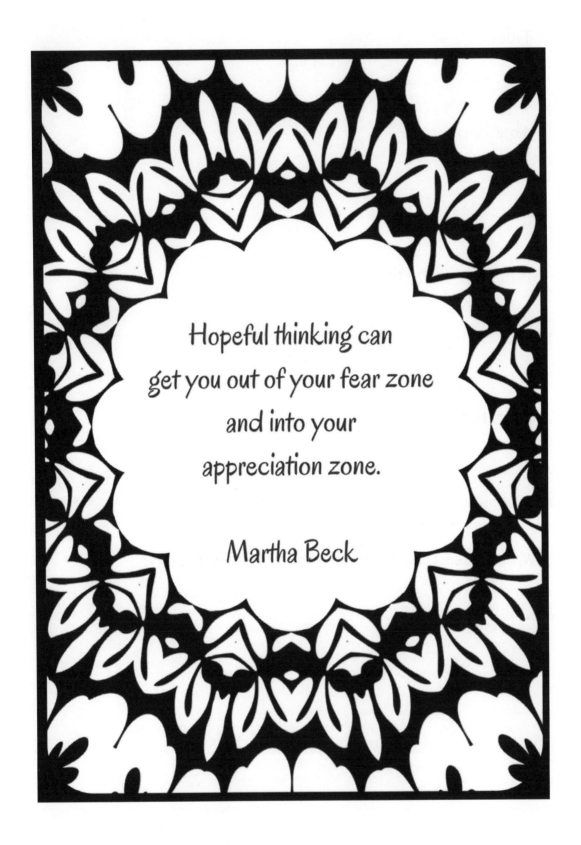

Hopeful thinking can
get you out of your fear zone
and into your
appreciation zone.

Martha Beck

Today's Date:_____

Title:

What happened:

How I felt at the time:

How I felt later:

What caused this to happen in the way that it did?

Nature's beauty is a gift
that cultivates
appreciation and gratitude.

Louie Schwartzberg

Today's Date:_____

Title:

What happened:

How I felt at the time:

How I felt later:

What caused this to happen in the way that it did?

17

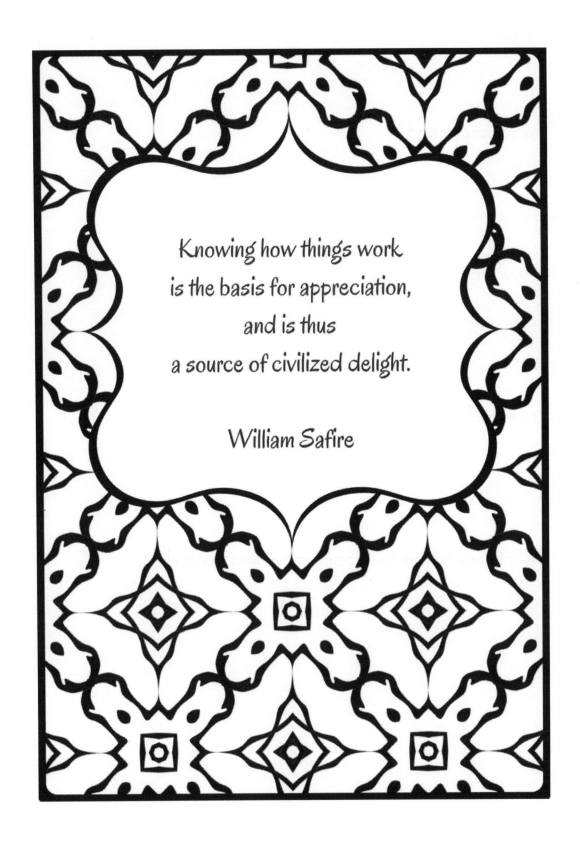

Knowing how things work
is the basis for appreciation,
and is thus
a source of civilized delight.

William Safire

Today's Date:_____

Title:

What happened:

How I felt at the time:

How I felt later:

What caused this to happen in the way that it did?

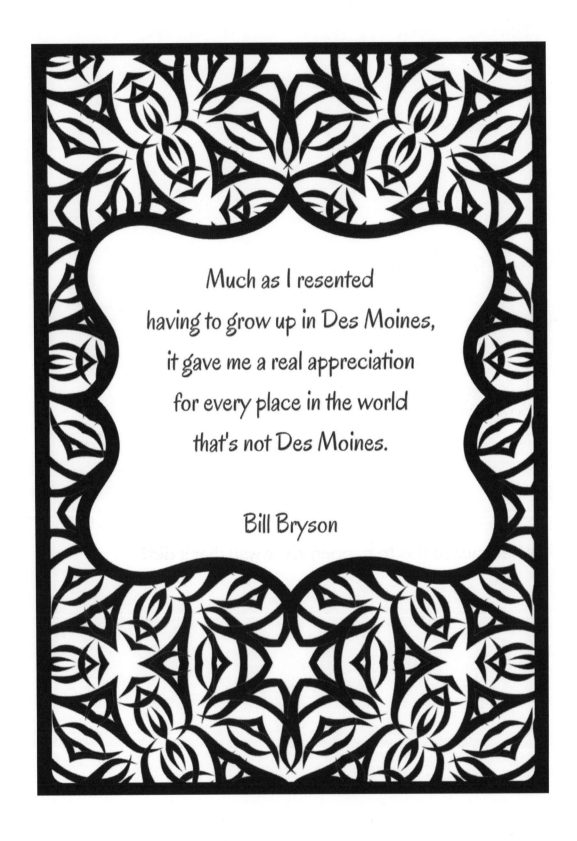

Much as I resented
having to grow up in Des Moines,
it gave me a real appreciation
for every place in the world
that's not Des Moines.

Bill Bryson

Today's Date:_____

Title:

What happened:

How I felt at the time:

How I felt later:

What caused this to happen in the way that it did?

People don't appreciate
their intestines
until something goes wrong.
But I always hope that people gain
a little appreciation for their guts.

Mary Roach

Title:

What happened:

How I felt at the time:

How I felt later:

What caused this to happen in the way that it did?

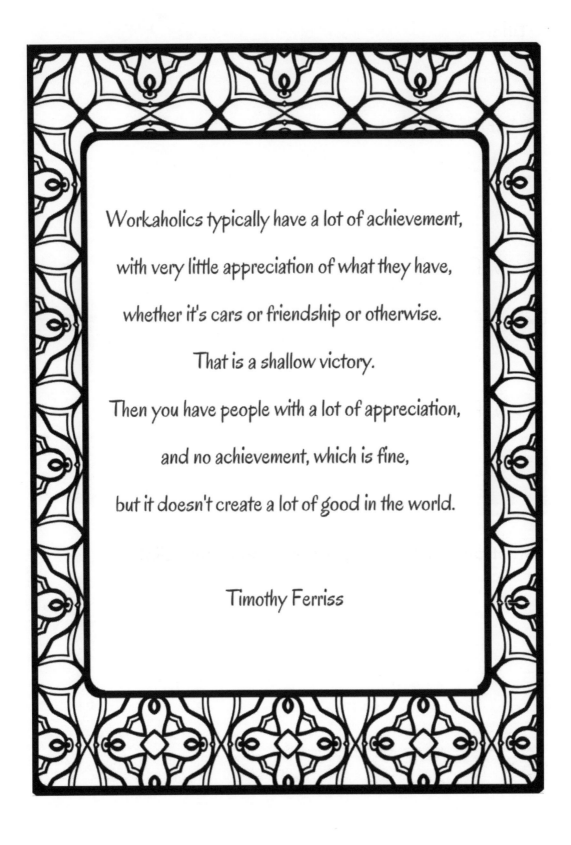

Workaholics typically have a lot of achievement,

with very little appreciation of what they have,

whether it's cars or friendship or otherwise.

That is a shallow victory.

Then you have people with a lot of appreciation,

and no achievement, which is fine,

but it doesn't create a lot of good in the world.

Timothy Ferriss

Title:

What happened:

How I felt at the time:

How I felt later:

What caused this to happen in the way that it did?

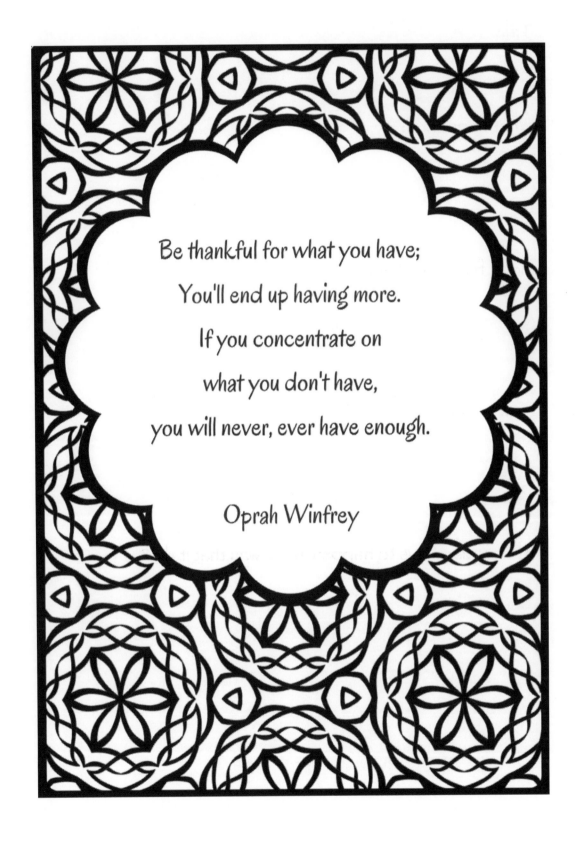

Be thankful for what you have;

You'll end up having more.

If you concentrate on

what you don't have,

you will never, ever have enough.

Oprah Winfrey

Title:

What happened:

How I felt at the time:

How I felt later:

What caused this to happen in the way that it did?

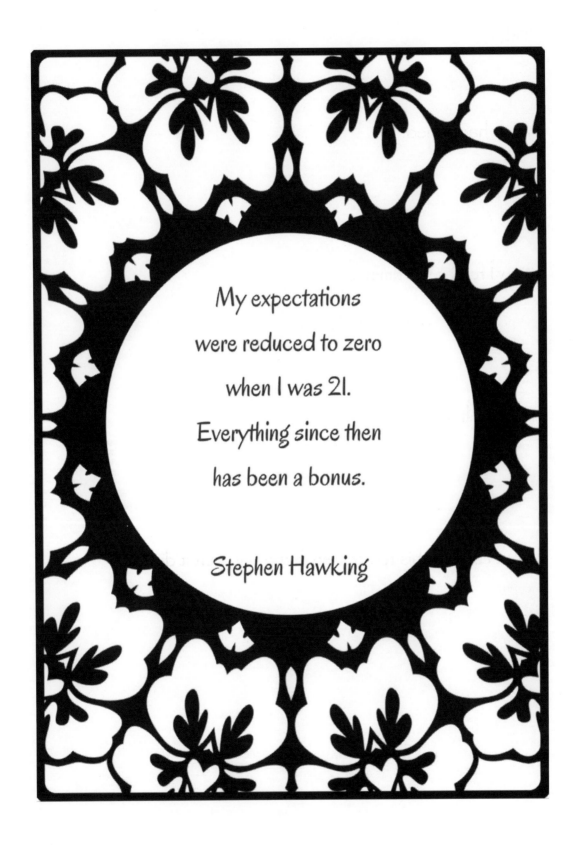

My expectations
were reduced to zero
when I was 21.
Everything since then
has been a bonus.

Stephen Hawking

Today's Date:_____

Title:

What happened:

How I felt at the time:

How I felt later:

What caused this to happen in the way that it did?

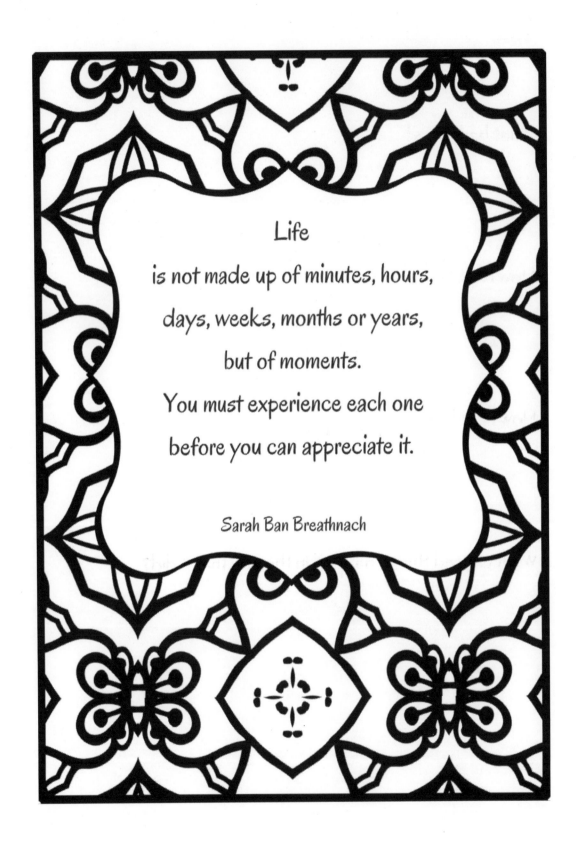

Life

is not made up of minutes, hours,

days, weeks, months or years,

but of moments.

You must experience each one

before you can appreciate it.

Sarah Ban Breathnach

Title:

What happened:

How I felt at the time:

How I felt later:

What caused this to happen in the way that it did?

I would rather
be able to appreciate things
I cannot have,
than to have things
I cannot appreciate.

Elbert Hubbard

Today's Date:_____

Title:

What happened:

How I felt at the time:

How I felt later:

What caused this to happen in the way that it did?

Just because
it isn't perfect
doesn't mean
it isn't awesome.

M.R. Mathias

Title:

What happened:

How I felt at the time:

How I felt later:

What caused this to happen in the way that it did?

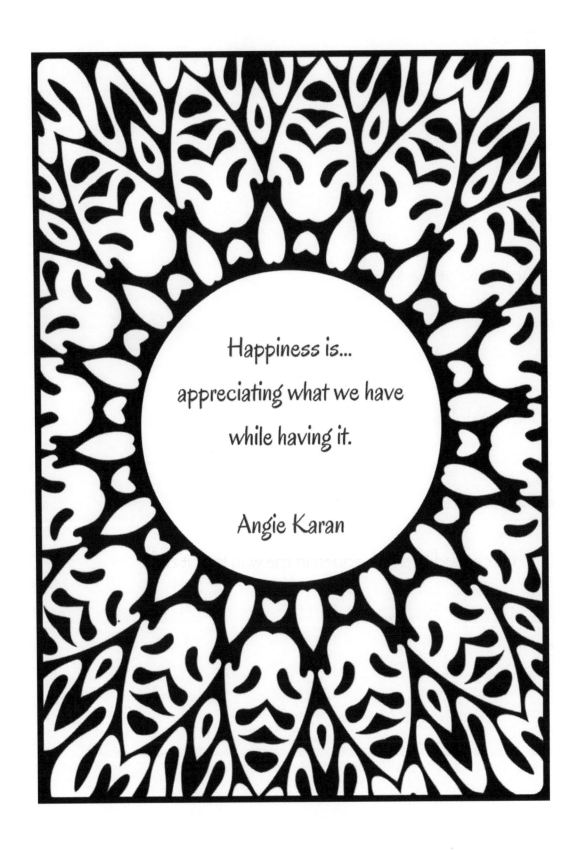

Happiness is...

appreciating what we have

while having it.

Angie Karan

Title:

What happened:

How I felt at the time:

How I felt later:

What caused this to happen in the way that it did?

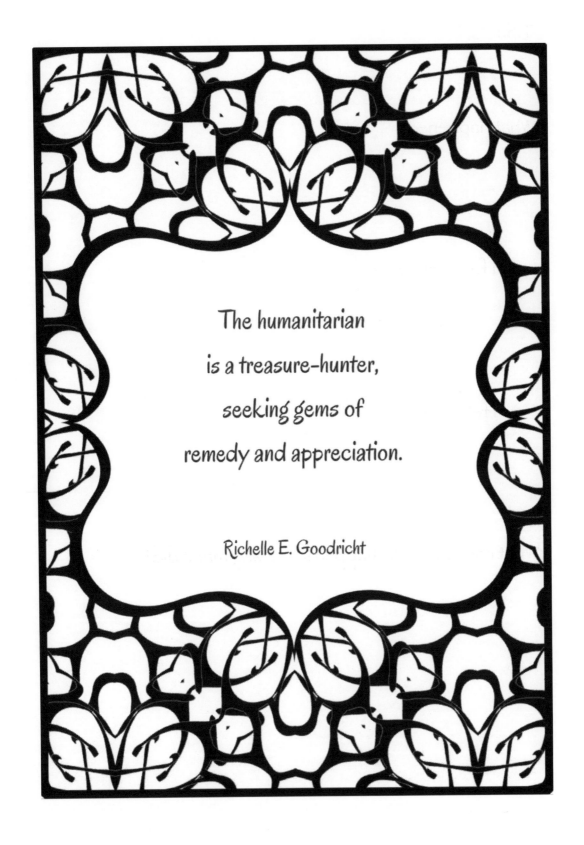

The humanitarian

is a treasure-hunter,

seeking gems of

remedy and appreciation.

Richelle E. Goodricht

Title:

What happened:

How I felt at the time:

How I felt later:

What caused this to happen in the way that it did?

The happiest people
are not those with the best
or most things,
but those who most appreciate
what they have.

Oliver Gaspirtz

Title:

What happened:

How I felt at the time:

How I felt later:

What caused this to happen in the way that it did?

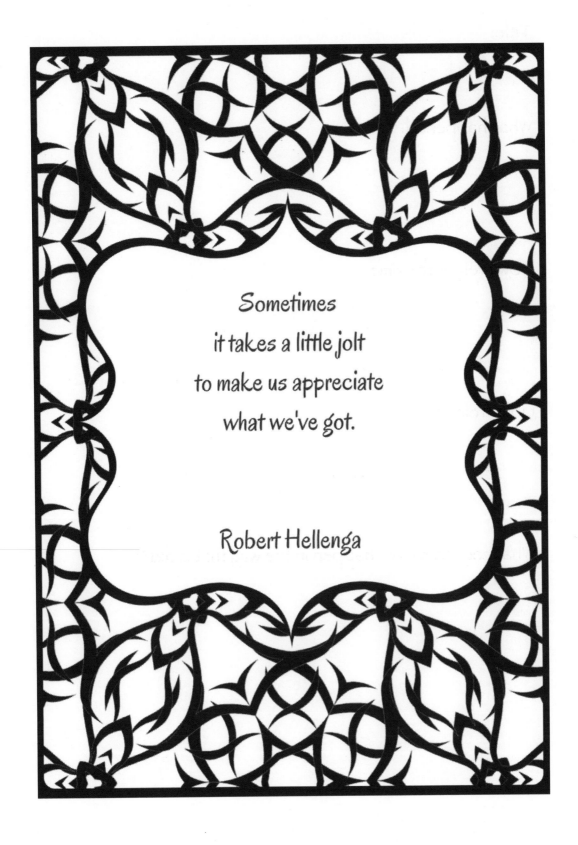

Sometimes
it takes a little jolt
to make us appreciate
what we've got.

Robert Hellenga

Today's Date:_____.

Title:

What happened:

How I felt at the time:

How I felt later:

What caused this to happen in the way that it did?

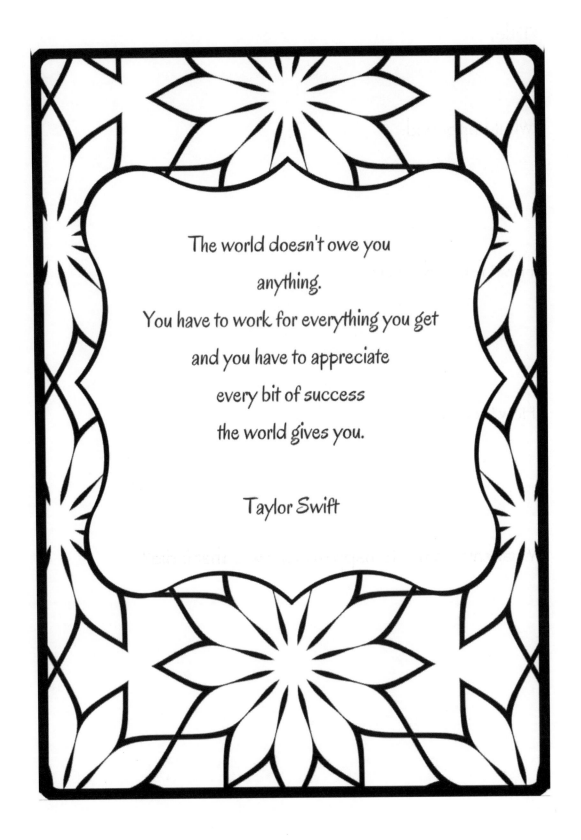

The world doesn't owe you
anything.
You have to work for everything you get
and you have to appreciate
every bit of success
the world gives you.

Taylor Swift

Title:

What happened:

How I felt at the time:

How I felt later:

What caused this to happen in the way that it did?

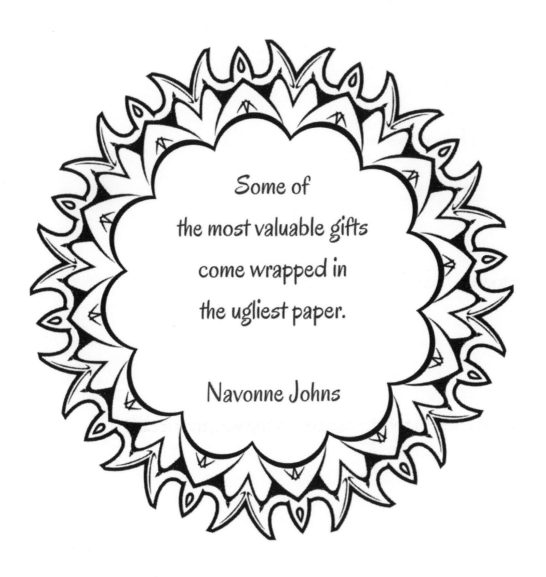

Some of
the most valuable gifts
come wrapped in
the ugliest paper.

Navonne Johns

Title:

What happened:

How I felt at the time:

How I felt later:

What caused this to happen in the way that it did?

There is just

as much beauty

visible to us in the landscape

as we are prepared to appreciate,

and not a grain more.

Henry David Thoreau

Title:

What happened:

How I felt at the time:

How I felt later:

What caused this to happen in the way that it did?

The whole problem with people is
they know what matters,
but they don't choose it.

Sue Monk Kidd

Title:

What happened:

How I felt at the time:

How I felt later:

What caused this to happen in the way that it did?

Our task
and challenge as human beings
is to appreciate, in the same instant,
both the infinite significance
and absolute insignificance
of life.

Eric Micha'el Leventhal

Today's Date:_____

Title:

What happened:

How I felt at the time:

How I felt later:

What caused this to happen in the way that it did?

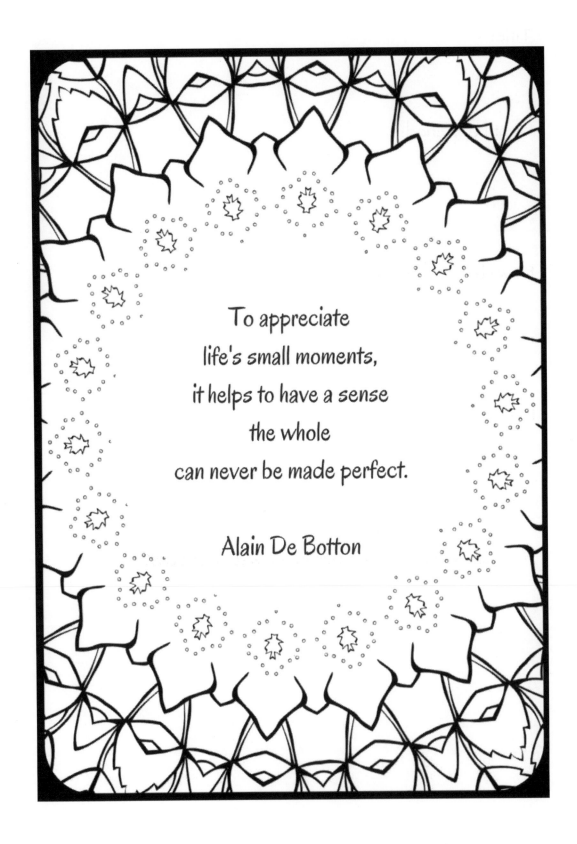

To appreciate
life's small moments,
it helps to have a sense
the whole
can never be made perfect.

Alain De Botton

Today's Date:_____

Title:

What happened:

How I felt at the time:

How I felt later:

What caused this to happen in the way that it did?

Never pass up an opportunity
to speak a kind word of appreciation.
There are six billion people on the planet,
and 5.9 billion of them
go to bed every night starving
for one honest word of appreciation.

Matthew Kelly

Today's Date:_____

Title:

What happened:

How I felt at the time:

How I felt later:

What caused this to happen in the way that it did?

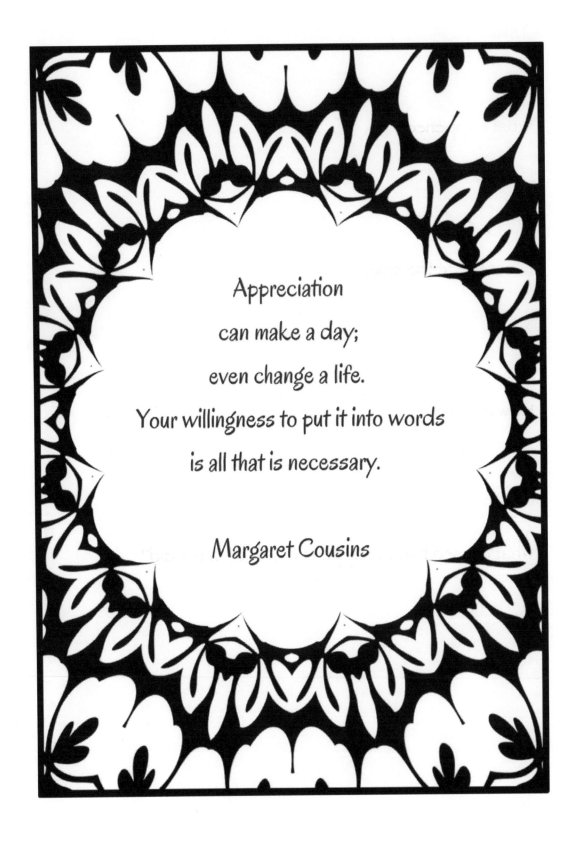

Appreciation

can make a day;

even change a life.

Your willingness to put it into words

is all that is necessary.

Margaret Cousins

Title:

What happened:

How I felt at the time:

How I felt later:

What caused this to happen in the way that it did?

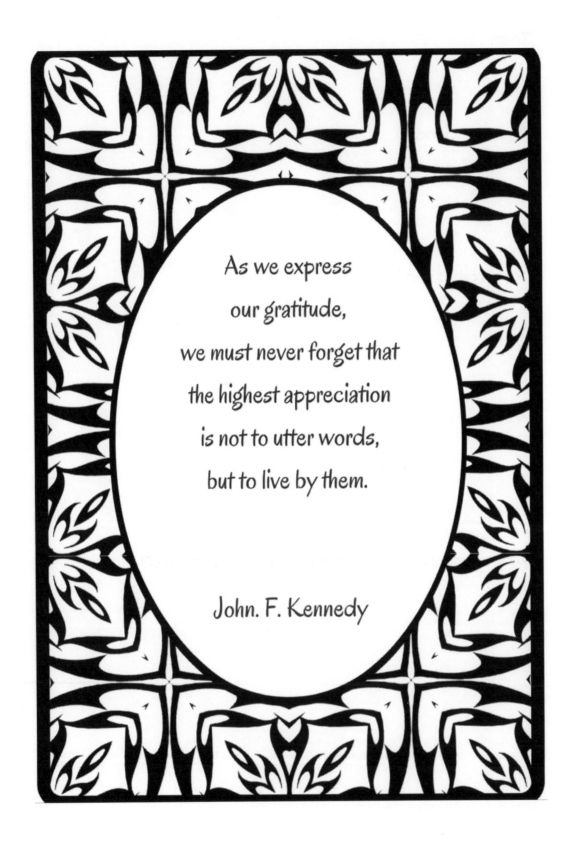

As we express

our gratitude,

we must never forget that

the highest appreciation

is not to utter words,

but to live by them.

John. F. Kennedy

Today's Date:_____

Title:

What happened:

How I felt at the time:

How I felt later:

What caused this to happen in the way that it did?

The invariable mark
of wisdom
is to see the miraculous
in the common.

Ralph Waldo Emerson

Today's Date:_____

Title:

What happened:

How I felt at the time:

How I felt later:

What caused this to happen in the way that it did?

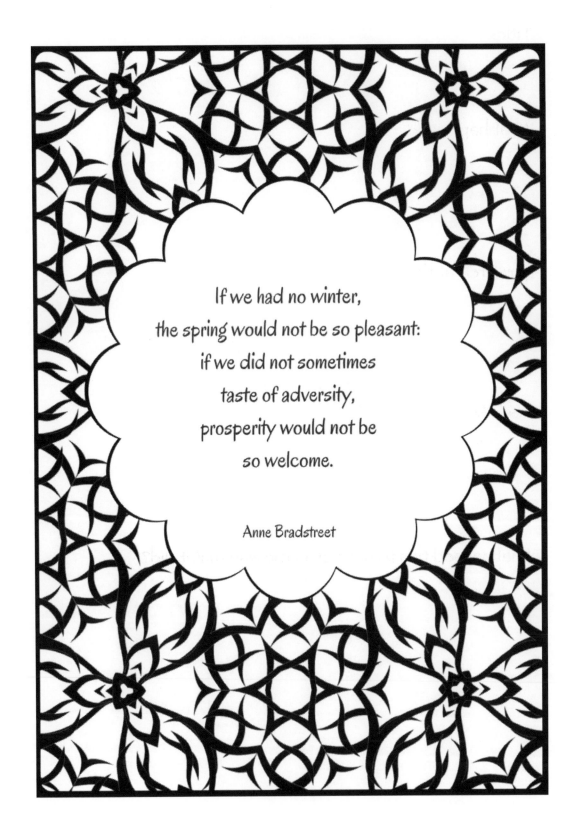

If we had no winter,
the spring would not be so pleasant:
if we did not sometimes
taste of adversity,
prosperity would not be
so welcome.

Anne Bradstreet

Title:

What happened:

How I felt at the time:

How I felt later:

What caused this to happen in the way that it did?

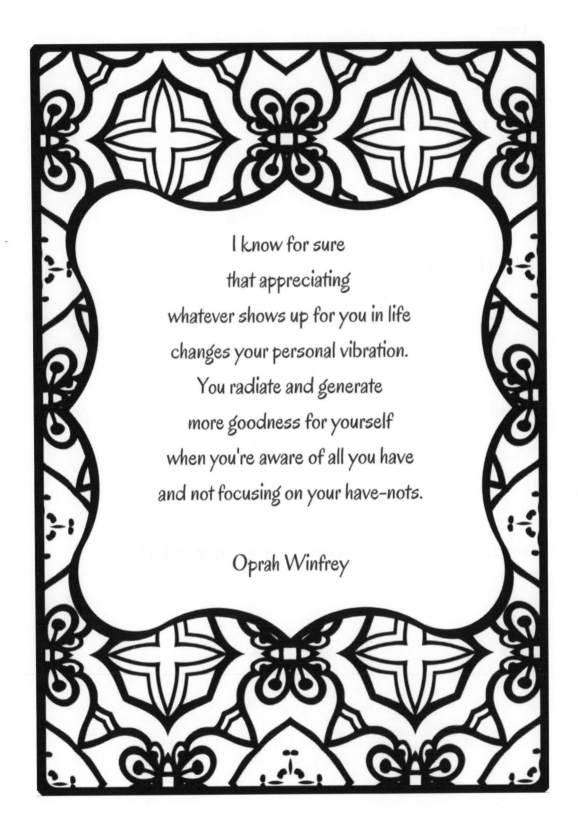

I know for sure
that appreciating
whatever shows up for you in life
changes your personal vibration.
You radiate and generate
more goodness for yourself
when you're aware of all you have
and not focusing on your have-nots.

Oprah Winfrey

Title:

What happened:

How I felt at the time:

How I felt later:

What caused this to happen in the way that it did?

Sometimes we fight who we are,
struggling against ourselves
and our natures.
But we must learn to accept who we are
and appreciate who we become.
We must love ourselves
for what and who we are,
and believe in our talents.

Harley King

Title:

What happened:

How I felt at the time:

How I felt later:

What caused this to happen in the way that it did?

There's a sunrise
and a sunset every single day,
and they're absolutely free.
Don't miss so many of them.

Jo Walton

Title:

What happened:

How I felt at the time:

How I felt later:

What caused this to happen in the way that it did?

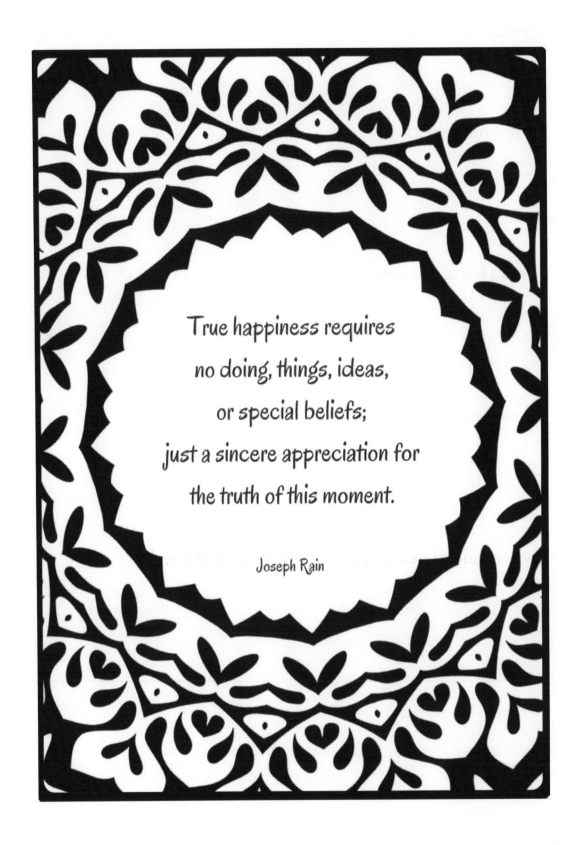

True happiness requires
no doing, things, ideas,
or special beliefs;
just a sincere appreciation for
the truth of this moment.

Joseph Rain

Today's Date:_____

Title:

What happened:

How I felt at the time:

How I felt later:

What caused this to happen in the way that it did?

Practice appreciation for
who you are and what you have…
and allow your life to unfold
in the most amazing way.

Millen Livis

Title:

What happened:

How I felt at the time:

How I felt later:

What caused this to happen in the way that it did?

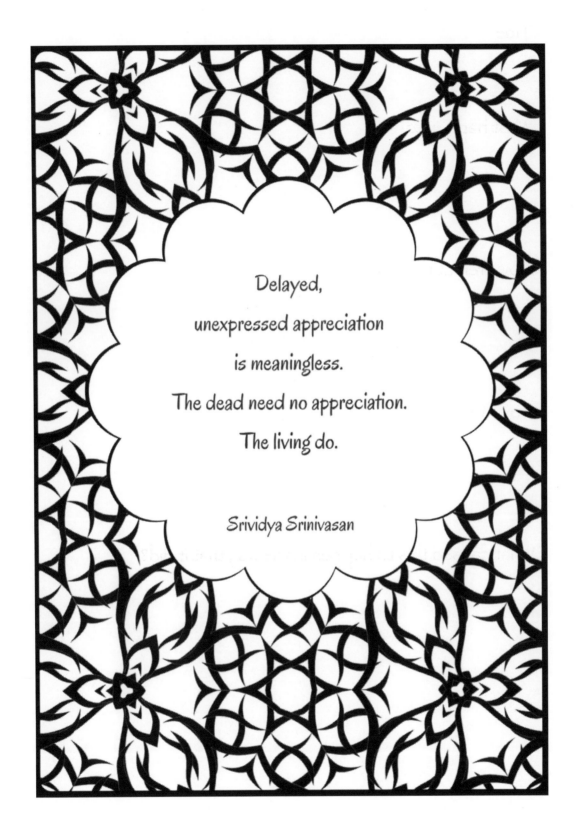

Delayed,

unexpressed appreciation

is meaningless.

The dead need no appreciation.

The living do.

Srividya Srinivasan

Title:

What happened:

How I felt at the time:

How I felt later:

What caused this to happen in the way that it did?

True wisdom

is being able to say

'it is what it is'

with a smile

of celebratory wonder

on your face.

Eric Micha'el Leventhal

Today's Date:_____

Title:

What happened:

How I felt at the time:

How I felt later:

What caused this to happen in the way that it did?

Being able to appreciate
who we are and what we have
in the now
is an easy way to journey
through this life.

Raphael Zernoff

Today's Date:_____

Title:

What happened:

How I felt at the time:

How I felt later:

What caused this to happen in the way that it did?

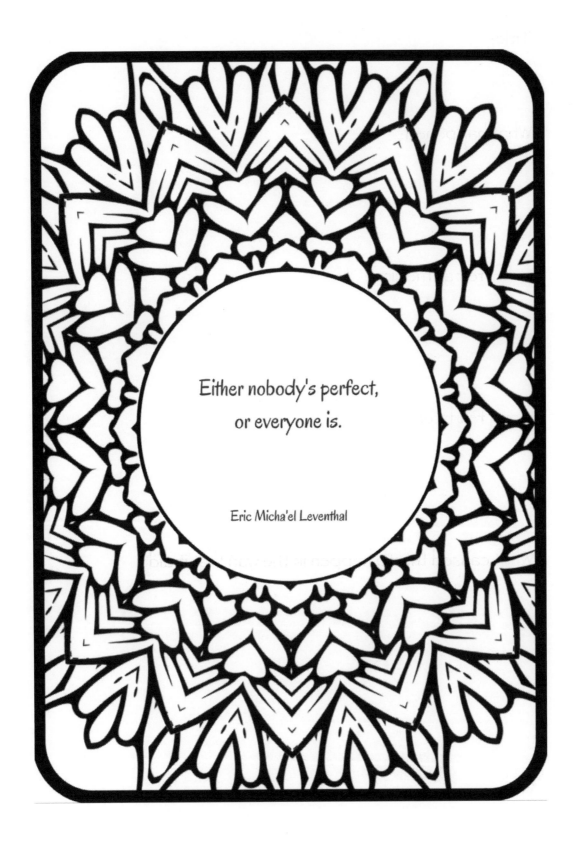

Either nobody's perfect,

or everyone is.

Eric Micha'el Leventhal

Today's Date:_____

Title:

What happened:

How I felt at the time:

How I felt later:

What caused this to happen in the way that it did?

The moment one gives
close attention to anything,
even a blade of grass,
it becomes a mysterious, awesome,
indescribably magnificent world
in itself.

Henry Miller

Title:

What happened:

How I felt at the time:

How I felt later:

What caused this to happen in the way that it did?

People always complain
that they can't do this
and they can't do that.
If we look at our lives
and concentrate on
things that we don't have
or wish to have,
that doesn't change the circumstances.
The truth is that we have to focus on
what we have
and make the best out of it.

Nick Vujicic

Today's Date:_____

Title:

What happened:

How I felt at the time:

How I felt later:

What caused this to happen in the way that it did?

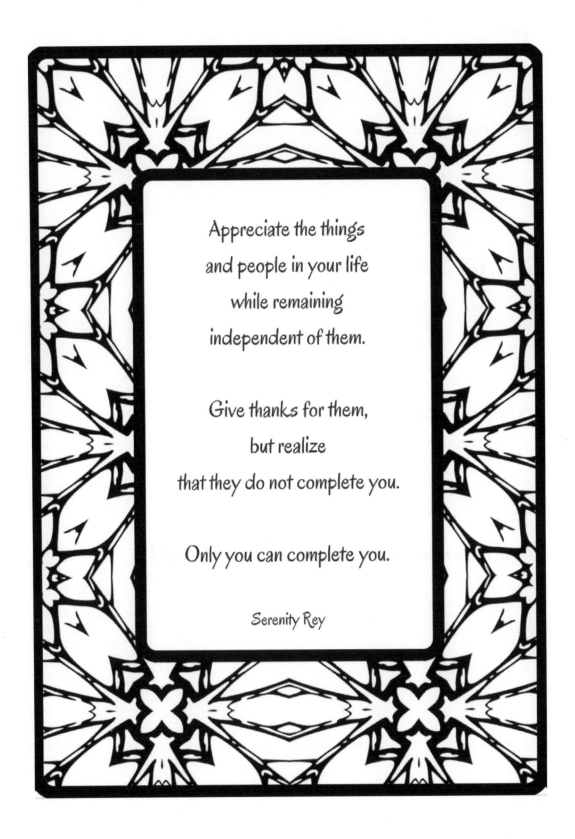

Appreciate the things
and people in your life
while remaining
independent of them.

Give thanks for them,
but realize
that they do not complete you.

Only you can complete you.

Serenity Rey

Today's Date:_____

Title:

What happened:

How I felt at the time:

How I felt later:

What caused this to happen in the way that it did?

The best way to
appreciate your job is
to imagine yourself
without one.

Oscar Wilde

Today's Date:_____

Title:

What happened:

How I felt at the time:

How I felt later:

What caused this to happen in the way that it did?

The greatest of all gifts
is the power to estimate things
at their true worth.

Francois de la Rochefoucauld

Today's Date:_____

Title:

What happened:

How I felt at the time:

How I felt later:

What caused this to happen in the way that it did?

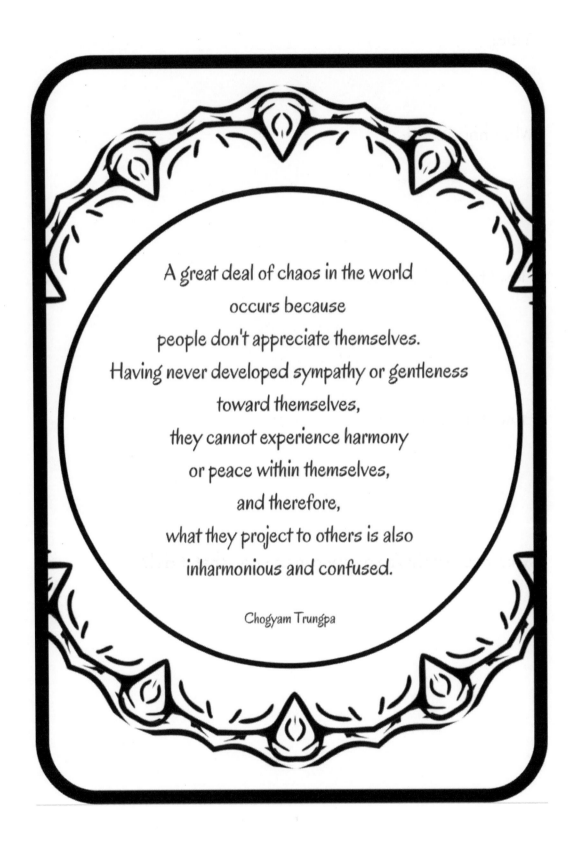

A great deal of chaos in the world
occurs because
people don't appreciate themselves.
Having never developed sympathy or gentleness
toward themselves,
they cannot experience harmony
or peace within themselves,
and therefore,
what they project to others is also
inharmonious and confused.

Chogyam Trungpa

Today's Date:_____

Title:

What happened:

How I felt at the time:

How I felt later:

What caused this to happen in the way that it did?

Being truly thankful

makes you infinitely more resourceful.

By sincerely appreciating what you have,

you find new and valuable ways

to make use of it.

Ralph Marston

Today's Date:_____

Title:

What happened:

How I felt at the time:

How I felt later:

What caused this to happen in the way that it did?

Even after all this time,

the sun never says to the earth,

'You owe me.'

Look what happens with a love like that.

It lights the whole sky.

Hafiz of Persia

Today's Date:_____

Title:

What happened:

How I felt at the time:

How I felt later:

What caused this to happen in the way that it did?

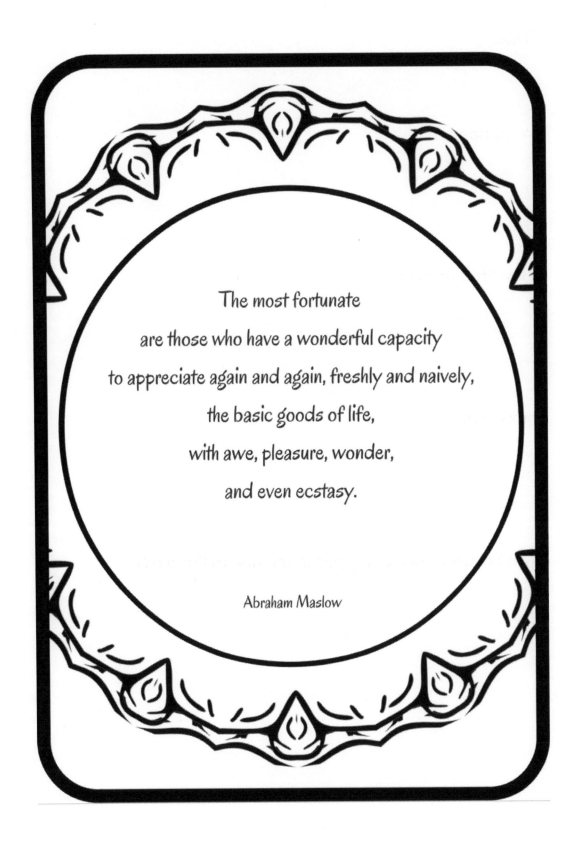

The most fortunate

are those who have a wonderful capacity

to appreciate again and again, freshly and naively,

the basic goods of life,

with awe, pleasure, wonder,

and even ecstasy.

Abraham Maslow

Today's Date:_____

Title:

What happened:

How I felt at the time:

How I felt later:

What caused this to happen in the way that it did?

To appreciate
the balance in life,
you have to lose it
every now and then.

Rod Williams

Today's Date:_____

Title:

What happened:

How I felt at the time:

How I felt later:

What caused this to happen in the way that it did?

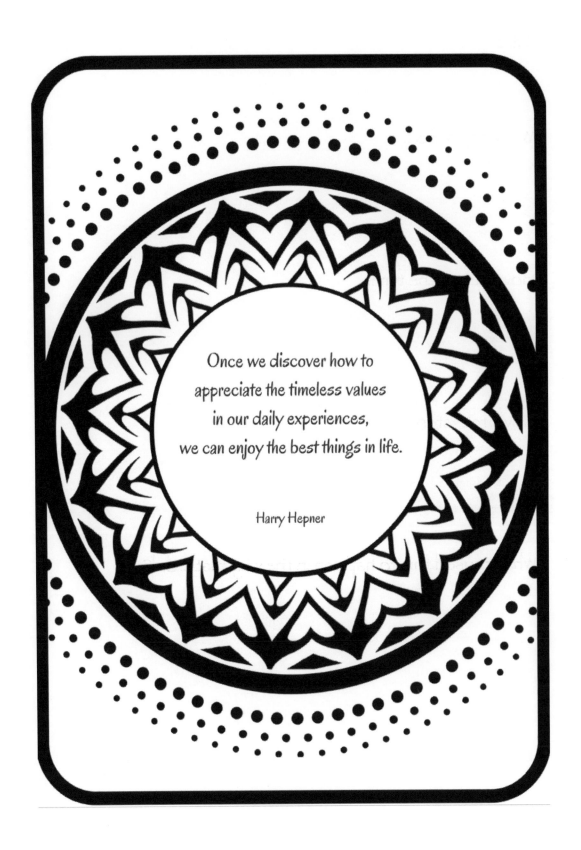

Once we discover how to
appreciate the timeless values
in our daily experiences,
we can enjoy the best things in life.

Harry Hepner

Today's Date:_____

Title:

What happened:

How I felt at the time:

How I felt later:

What caused this to happen in the way that it did?

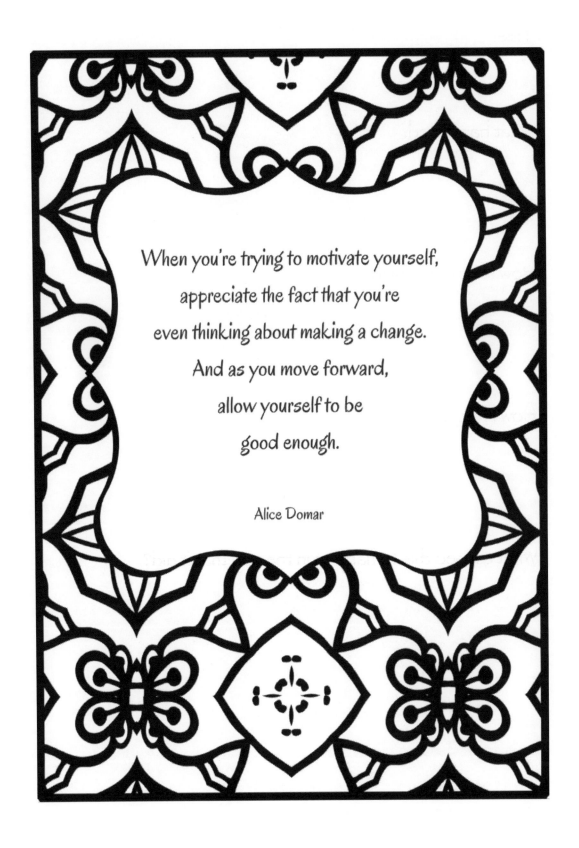

When you're trying to motivate yourself,

appreciate the fact that you're

even thinking about making a change.

And as you move forward,

allow yourself to be

good enough.

Alice Domar

Today's Date:_____

Title:

What happened:

How I felt at the time:

How I felt later:

What caused this to happen in the way that it did?

Live with intention.
Walk to the edge.
Listen hard.
Practice wellness.
Play with abandon.
Laugh.
Choose with no regret.
Appreciate your friends.
Continue to learn.
Do what you love.
Live as if this is all there is.

Mary Anne Radmacher

Today's Date:_____

Title:

What happened:

How I felt at the time:

How I felt later:

What caused this to happen in the way that it did?

The moment
an inspiring thought
enters your heart,
appreciate it as a dear guest
visiting you that day.

Rumi

Today's Date:_____

Title:

What happened:

How I felt at the time:

How I felt later:

What caused this to happen in the way that it did?

It takes patience
to appreciate domestic bliss;
volatile spirits prefer
unhappiness.

George Santayana

Title:

What happened:

How I felt at the time:

How I felt later:

What caused this to happen in the way that it did?

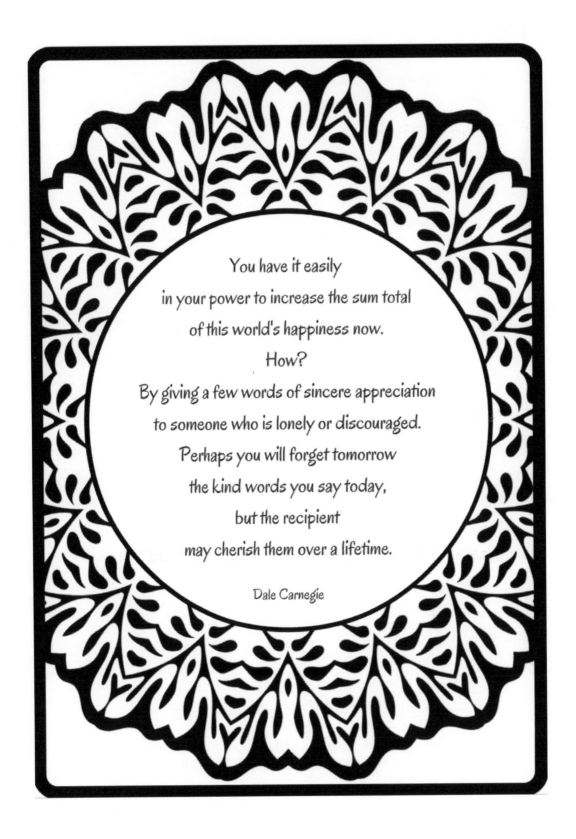

You have it easily

in your power to increase the sum total

of this world's happiness now.

How?

By giving a few words of sincere appreciation

to someone who is lonely or discouraged.

Perhaps you will forget tomorrow

the kind words you say today,

but the recipient

may cherish them over a lifetime.

Dale Carnegie

Title:

What happened:

How I felt at the time:

How I felt later:

What caused this to happen in the way that it did?

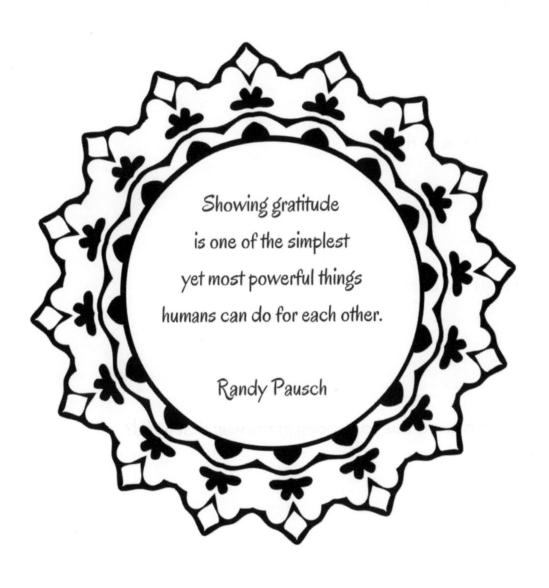

Showing gratitude
is one of the simplest
yet most powerful things
humans can do for each other.

Randy Pausch

Today's Date:_____

Title:

What happened:

How I felt at the time:

How I felt later:

What caused this to happen in the way that it did?

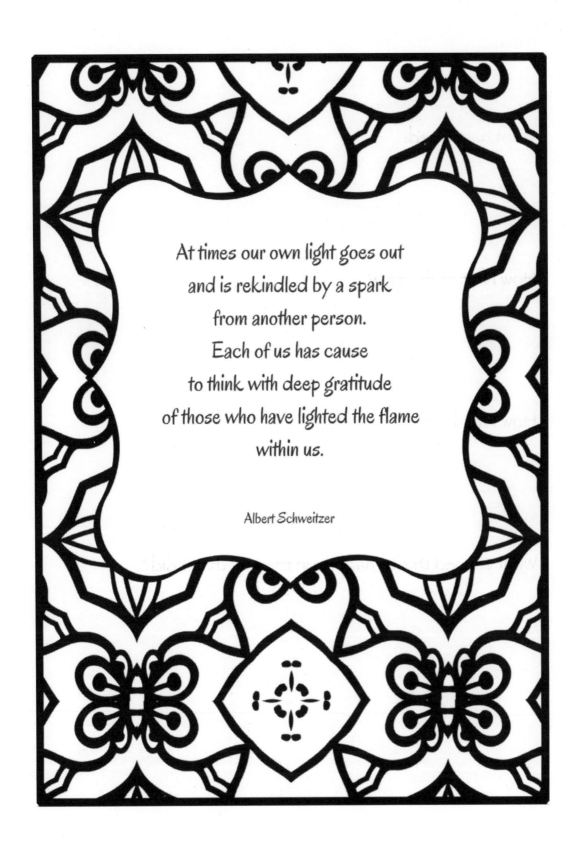

At times our own light goes out
and is rekindled by a spark
from another person.
Each of us has cause
to think with deep gratitude
of those who have lighted the flame
within us.

Albert Schweitzer

Today's Date:_____

Title:

What happened:

How I felt at the time:

How I felt later:

What caused this to happen in the way that it did?

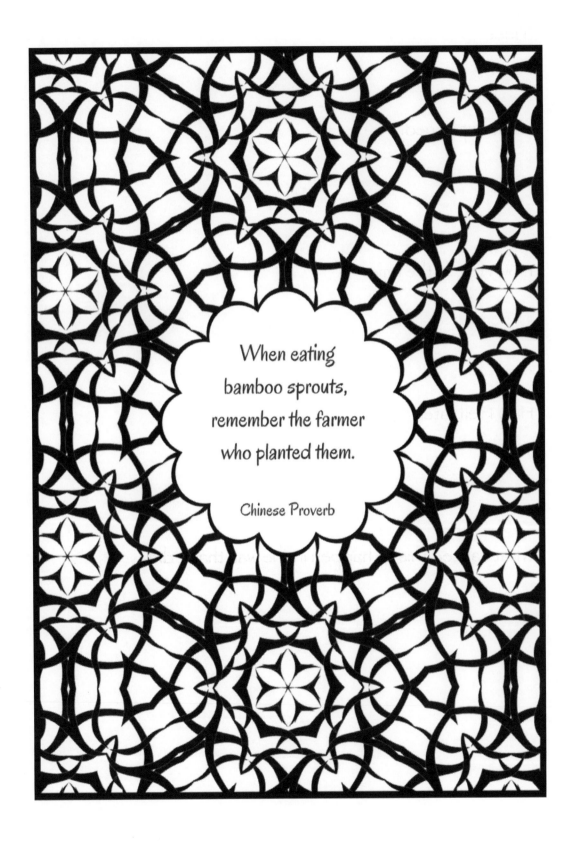

When eating
bamboo sprouts,
remember the farmer
who planted them.

Chinese Proverb

Today's Date:_____

Title:

What happened:

How I felt at the time:

How I felt later:

What caused this to happen in the way that it did?

Be glad of life
because it gives you the chance
to love, to work, to play,
and to look up at the stars.

Henry Van Dyke

Today's Date:_____

Title:

What happened:

How I felt at the time:

How I felt later:

What caused this to happen in the way that it did?

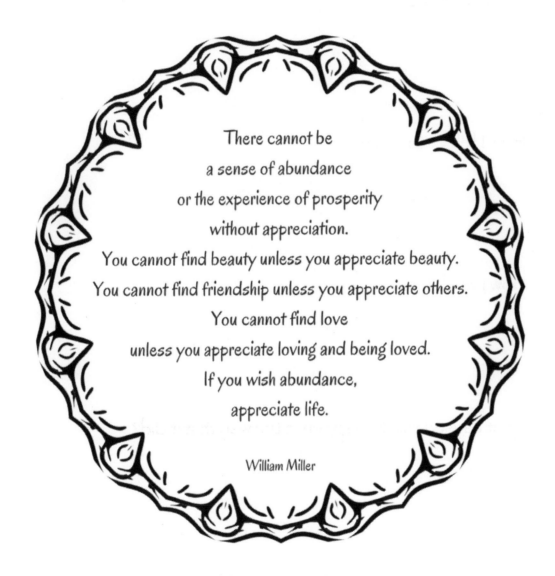

There cannot be
a sense of abundance
or the experience of prosperity
without appreciation.
You cannot find beauty unless you appreciate beauty.
You cannot find friendship unless you appreciate others.
You cannot find love
unless you appreciate loving and being loved.
If you wish abundance,
appreciate life.

William Miller

Today's Date:_____

Title:

What happened:

How I felt at the time:

How I felt later:

What caused this to happen in the way that it did?

Education

is the power to think clearly,

the power to act well

in the world's work,

and the power to appreciate life.

Brigham Young

Title:

What happened:

How I felt at the time:

How I felt later:

What caused this to happen in the way that it did?

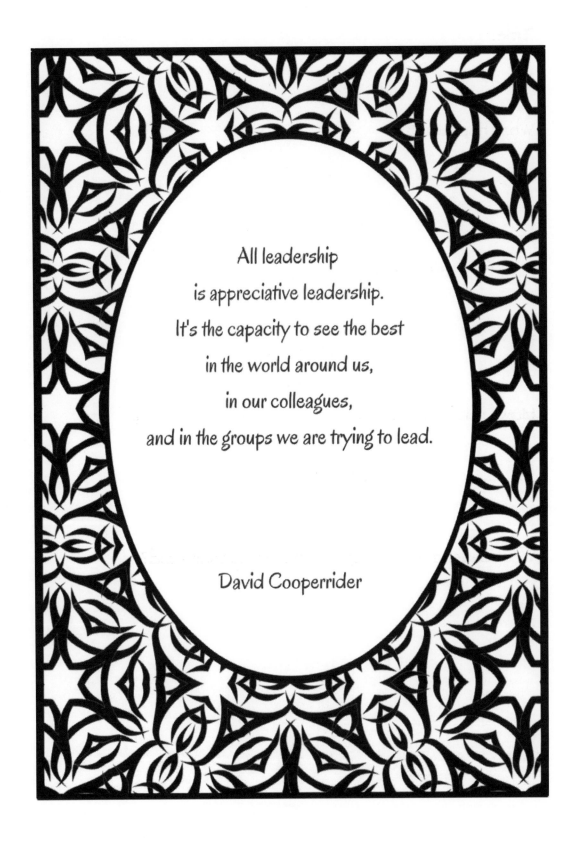

All leadership
is appreciative leadership.
It's the capacity to see the best
in the world around us,
in our colleagues,
and in the groups we are trying to lead.

David Cooperrider

128

Today's Date:_____

Title:

What happened:

How I felt at the time:

How I felt later:

What caused this to happen in the way that it did?

Be appreciative of
what's right with your life.
In your gratitude is power
to make it even better.

Ralph Marston

Today's Date:_____

Title:

What happened:

How I felt at the time:

How I felt later:

What caused this to happen in the way that it did?

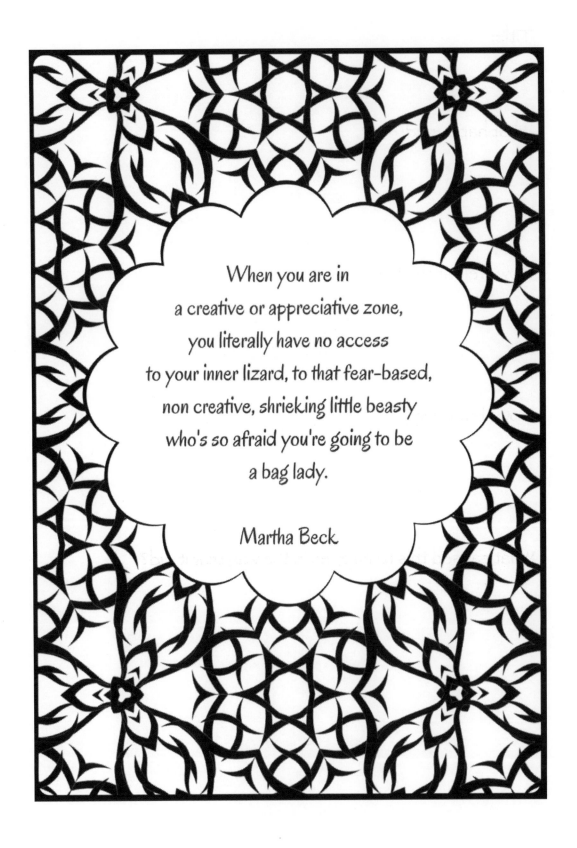

When you are in
a creative or appreciative zone,
you literally have no access
to your inner lizard, to that fear-based,
non creative, shrieking little beasty
who's so afraid you're going to be
a bag lady.

Martha Beck

132

Today's Date:_____

Title:

What happened:

How I felt at the time:

How I felt later:

What caused this to happen in the way that it did?

I believe that everything happens
for a reason.
People change
so that you can learn to let go,
things go wrong
so that you appreciate them
when they're right,
you believe lies so you eventually learn
to trust no one but yourself,
and sometimes good things fall apart
so better things can fall together.

Marilyn Monroe

Today's Date:_____

Title:

What happened:

How I felt at the time:

How I felt later:

What caused this to happen in the way that it did?

The two hardest tests
on the spiritual road
are the patience
to wait for the right moment
and the courage
not to be disappointed
with what we encounter.

Paulo Coelho

Today's Date:_____

Title:

What happened:

How I felt at the time:

How I felt later:

What caused this to happen in the way that it did?

Time and health
are two precious assets
that we don't recognize
and appreciate until
they have been depleted.

Denis Waitley

Title:

What happened:

How I felt at the time:

How I felt later:

What caused this to happen in the way that it did?

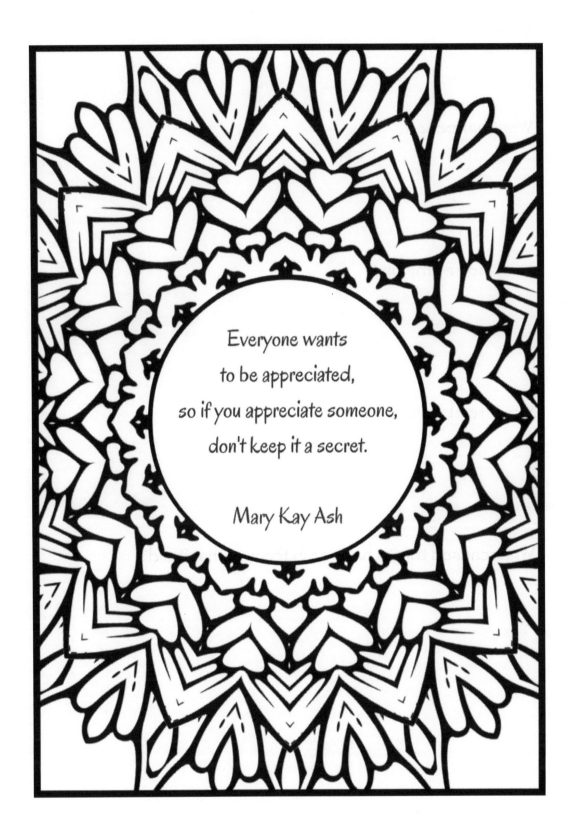

Everyone wants
to be appreciated,
so if you appreciate someone,
don't keep it a secret.

Mary Kay Ash

Today's Date:_____

Title:

What happened:

How I felt at the time:

How I felt later:

What caused this to happen in the way that it did?

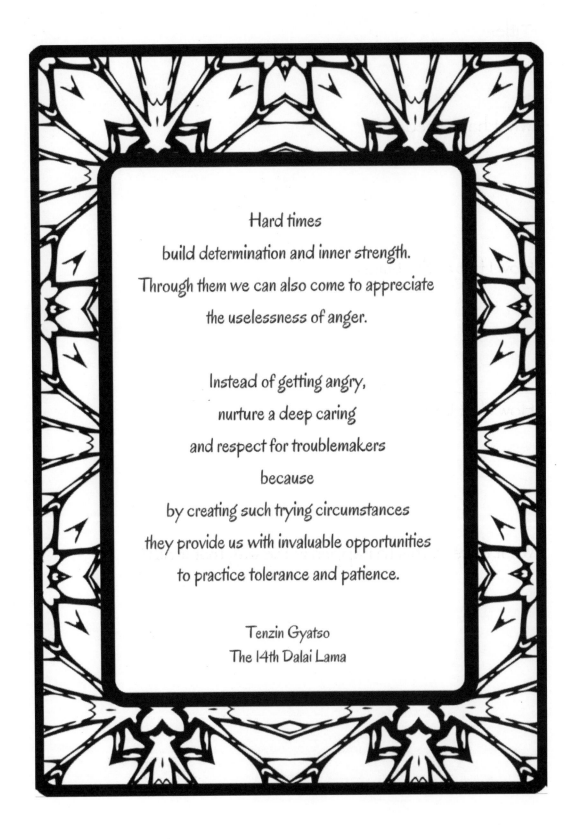

Hard times
build determination and inner strength.
Through them we can also come to appreciate
the uselessness of anger.

Instead of getting angry,
nurture a deep caring
and respect for troublemakers
because
by creating such trying circumstances
they provide us with invaluable opportunities
to practice tolerance and patience.

Tenzin Gyatso
The 14th Dalai Lama

Title:

What happened:

How I felt at the time:

How I felt later:

What caused this to happen in the way that it did?

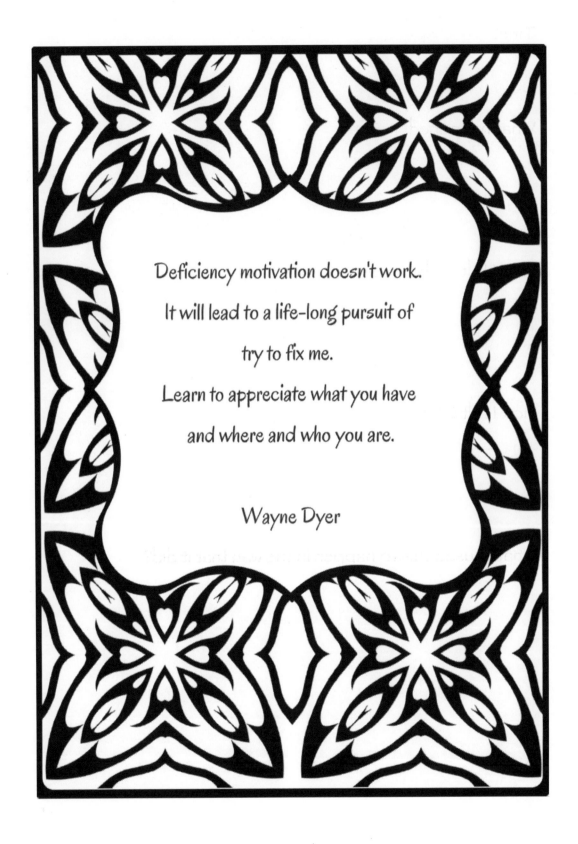

Deficiency motivation doesn't work.

It will lead to a life-long pursuit of

try to fix me.

Learn to appreciate what you have

and where and who you are.

Wayne Dyer

Title:

What happened:

How I felt at the time:

How I felt later:

What caused this to happen in the way that it did?

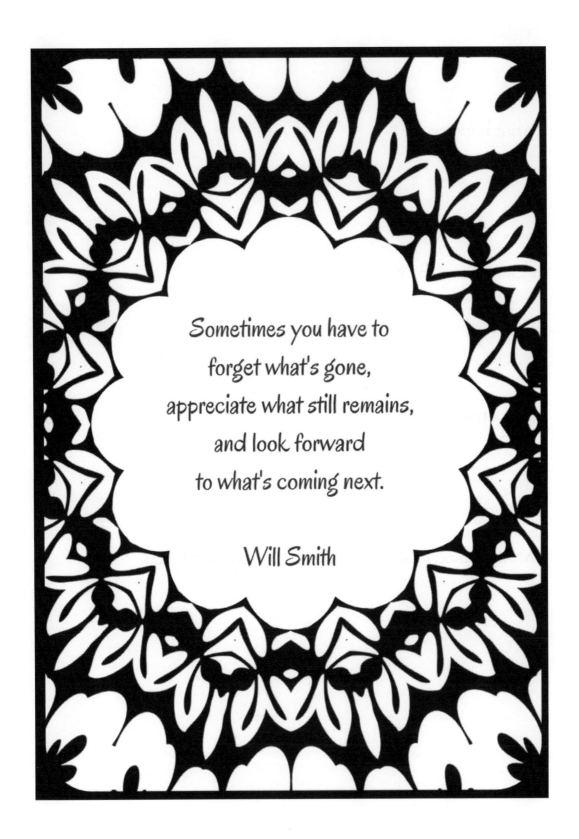

Sometimes you have to
forget what's gone,
appreciate what still remains,
and look forward
to what's coming next.

Will Smith

Today's Date:_____

Title:

What happened:

How I felt at the time:

How I felt later:

What caused this to happen in the way that it did?

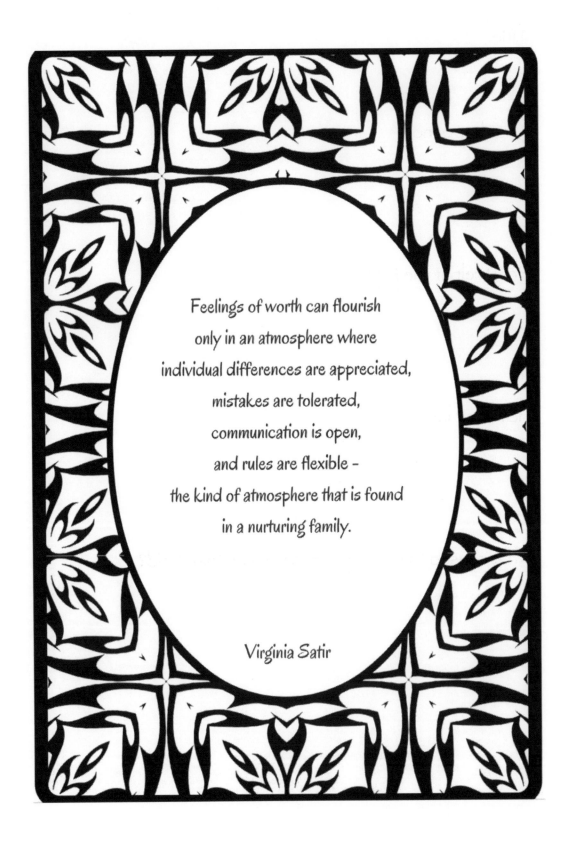

Feelings of worth can flourish
only in an atmosphere where
individual differences are appreciated,
mistakes are tolerated,
communication is open,
and rules are flexible -
the kind of atmosphere that is found
in a nurturing family.

Virginia Satir

Today's Date:_____

Title:

What happened:

How I felt at the time:

How I felt later:

What caused this to happen in the way that it did?

Unless we are willing
to encourage our children
to reconnect with
and appreciate
the natural world,
we can't expect them
to help protect
and care for it.

David Suzuki

Title:

What happened:

How I felt at the time:

How I felt later:

What caused this to happen in the way that it did?

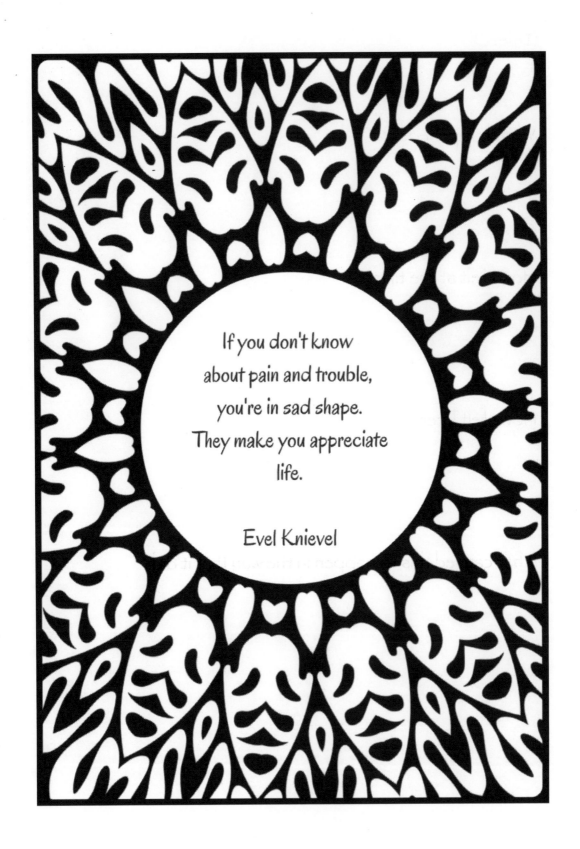

If you don't know
about pain and trouble,
you're in sad shape.
They make you appreciate
life.

Evel Knievel

Today's Date:_____

Title:

What happened:

How I felt at the time:

How I felt later:

What caused this to happen in the way that it did?

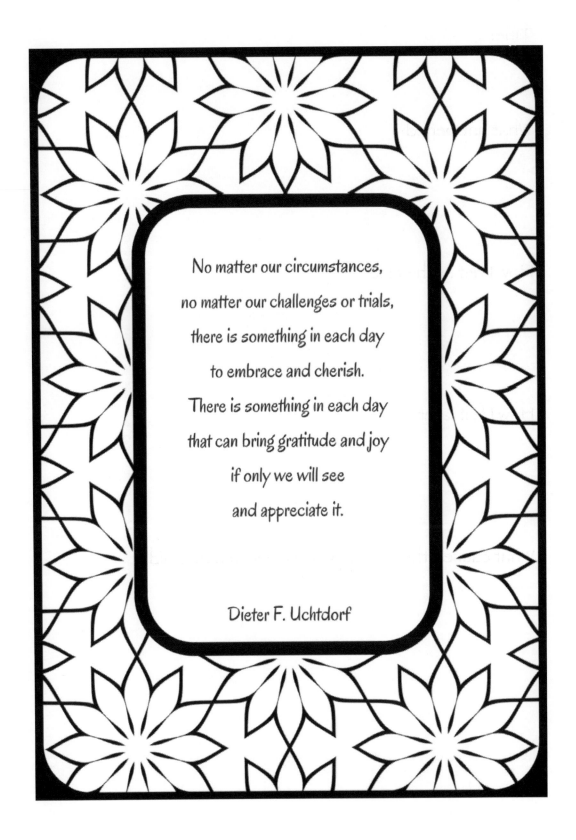

No matter our circumstances,

no matter our challenges or trials,

there is something in each day

to embrace and cherish.

There is something in each day

that can bring gratitude and joy

if only we will see

and appreciate it.

Dieter F. Uchtdorf

Today's Date:_____

Title:

What happened:

How I felt at the time:

How I felt later:

What caused this to happen in the way that it did?

Gratefulness for what is there
is one of the most powerful tools for
creating what is not yet there.
What does gratefulness mean?
It means you appreciate what is.
You value, you give attention to, you honor
whatever is here at this moment.

Eckhart Tolle

156

Today's Date:_____

Title:

What happened:

How I felt at the time:

How I felt later:

What caused this to happen in the way that it did?

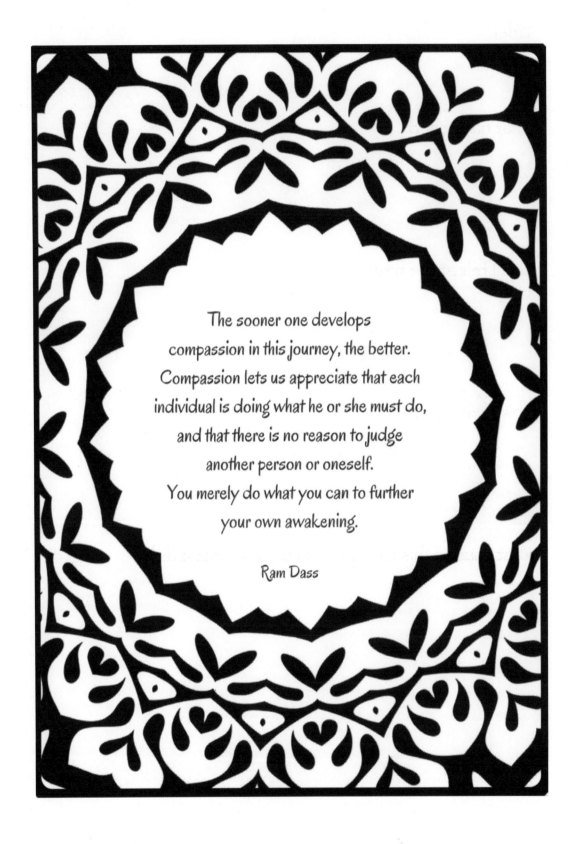

The sooner one develops
compassion in this journey, the better.
Compassion lets us appreciate that each
individual is doing what he or she must do,
and that there is no reason to judge
another person or oneself.
You merely do what you can to further
your own awakening.

Ram Dass

Today's Date:_____

Title:

What happened:

How I felt at the time:

How I felt later:

What caused this to happen in the way that it did?

To appreciate the sun
you gotta know what rain is.

J. Cole

Today's Date:_____

Title:

What happened:

How I felt at the time:

How I felt later:

What caused this to happen in the way that it did?

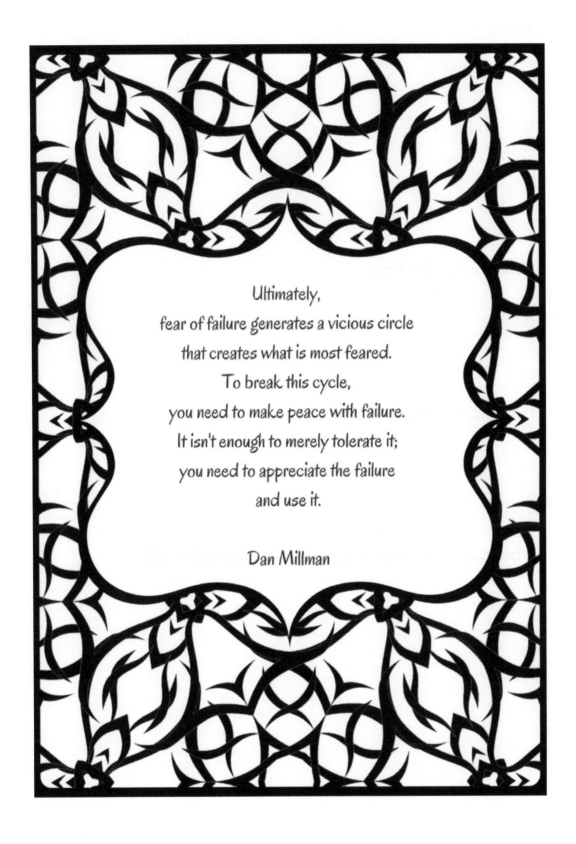

Ultimately,
fear of failure generates a vicious circle
that creates what is most feared.
To break this cycle,
you need to make peace with failure.
It isn't enough to merely tolerate it;
you need to appreciate the failure
and use it.

Dan Millman

Today's Date:_____

Title:

What happened:

How I felt at the time:

How I felt later:

What caused this to happen in the way that it did?

The value
we provide most to others
is the same value
we appreciate most
from others.

Simon Sinek

Today's Date:_____

Title:

What happened:

How I felt at the time:

How I felt later:

What caused this to happen in the way that it did?

If you don't appreciate
what you have in life right now,
whatever it is,
you will never realise your purpose.
Without appreciation,
you will never become strong enough
to respect yourself.

Caroline Myss

Title:

What happened:

How I felt at the time:

How I felt later:

What caused this to happen in the way that it did?

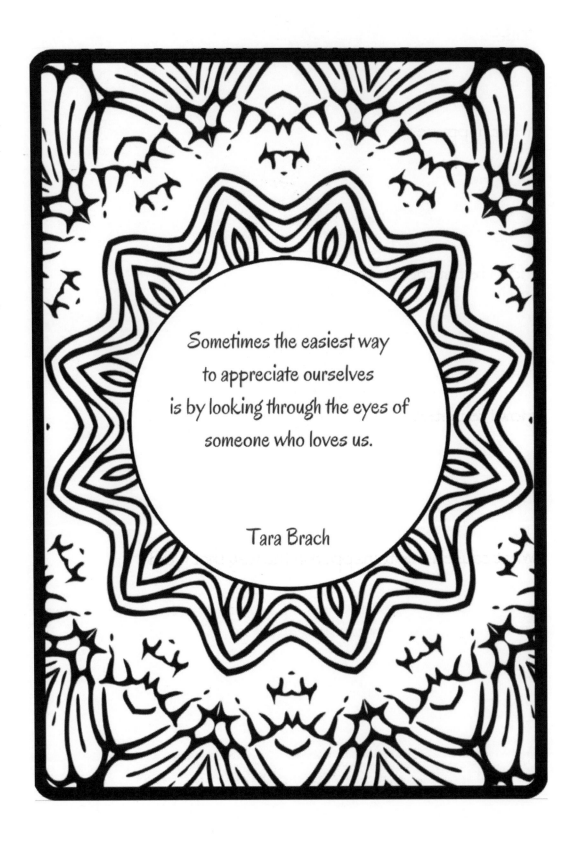

Sometimes the easiest way
to appreciate ourselves
is by looking through the eyes of
someone who loves us.

Tara Brach

Today's Date:_____

Title:

What happened:

How I felt at the time:

How I felt later:

What caused this to happen in the way that it did?

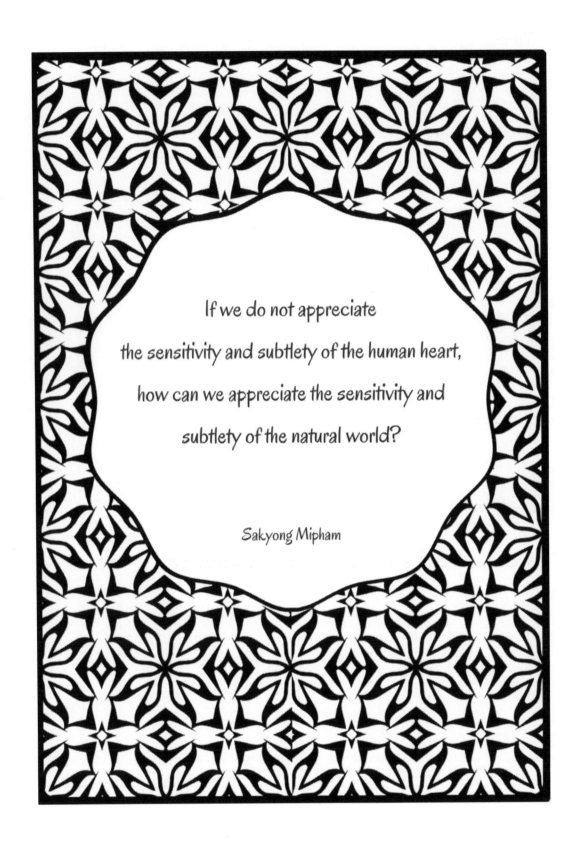

If we do not appreciate

the sensitivity and subtlety of the human heart,

how can we appreciate the sensitivity and

subtlety of the natural world?

Sakyong Mipham

Title:

What happened:

How I felt at the time:

How I felt later:

What caused this to happen in the way that it did?

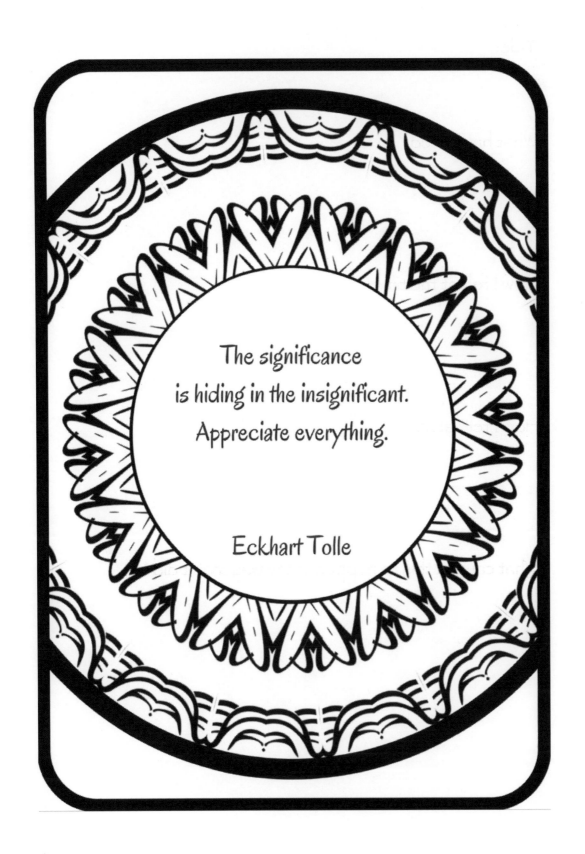

The significance
is hiding in the insignificant.
Appreciate everything.

Eckhart Tolle

Today's Date:_____

Title:

What happened:

How I felt at the time:

How I felt later:

What caused this to happen in the way that it did?

How do we keep our inner fire alive?

Two things, at minimum, are needed:

an ability to appreciate the positives in our life,

and a commitment to action.

Every day,

it's important to ask and answer these questions:

'What's good in my life?'

and

'What needs to be done?'

Nathaniel Branden

Today's Date:_____

Title:

What happened:

How I felt at the time:

How I felt later:

What caused this to happen in the way that it did?

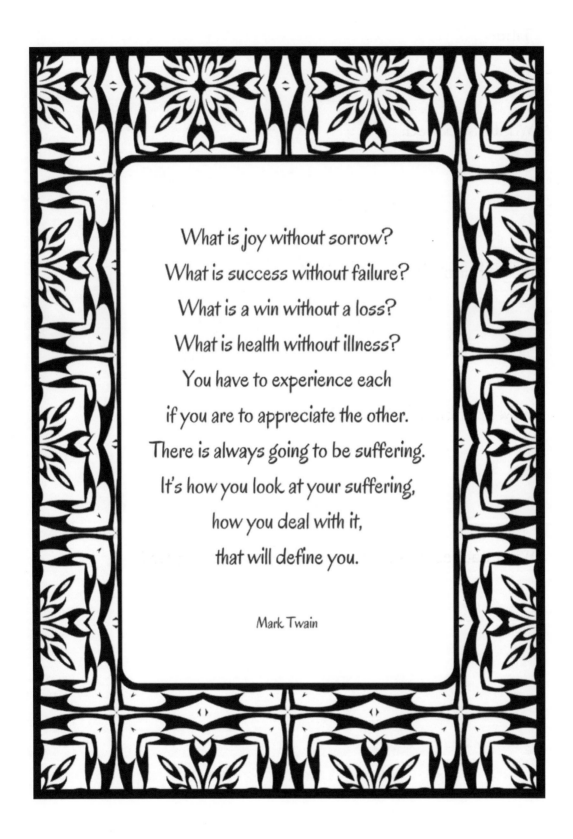

What is joy without sorrow?

What is success without failure?

What is a win without a loss?

What is health without illness?

You have to experience each

if you are to appreciate the other.

There is always going to be suffering.

It's how you look at your suffering,

how you deal with it,

that will define you.

Mark Twain

Today's Date:_____

Title:

What happened:

How I felt at the time:

How I felt later:

What caused this to happen in the way that it did?

If good things lasted forever,
would we appreciate how
precious they are?

Bill Watterson

Today's Date:_____

Title:

What happened:

How I felt at the time:

How I felt later:

What caused this to happen in the way that it did?

I'm grateful for being here,
for being able to think,
for being able to see,
for being able to taste,
for appreciating love –
for knowing that it exists
in a world so rife with vulgarity,
with brutality and violence,
and yet love exists.
I'm grateful to know
that it exists.

Maya Angelou

Title:

What happened:

How I felt at the time:

How I felt later:

What caused this to happen in the way that it did?

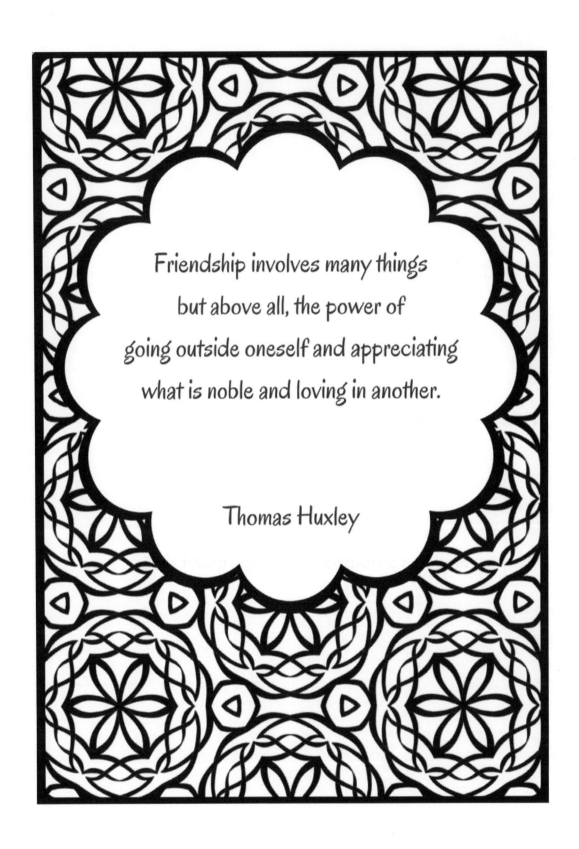

Friendship involves many things
but above all, the power of
going outside oneself and appreciating
what is noble and loving in another.

Thomas Huxley

Today's Date:_____

Title:

What happened:

How I felt at the time:

How I felt later:

What caused this to happen in the way that it did?

Don't be concerned
about others
not appreciating you.
Be concerned about your
not appreciating others.

Confucius

Title:

What happened:

How I felt at the time:

How I felt later:

What caused this to happen in the way that it did?

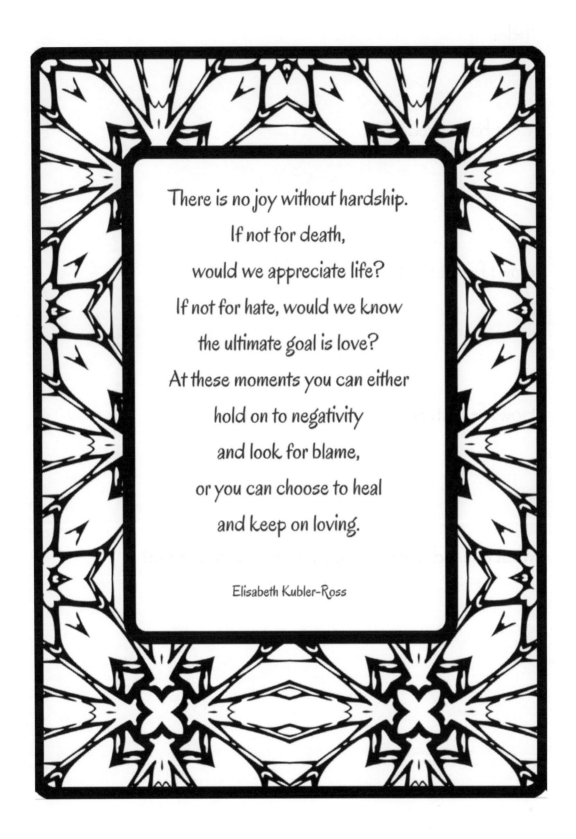

There is no joy without hardship.
If not for death,
would we appreciate life?
If not for hate, would we know
the ultimate goal is love?
At these moments you can either
hold on to negativity
and look for blame,
or you can choose to heal
and keep on loving.

Elisabeth Kubler-Ross

Today's Date:_____

Title:

What happened:

How I felt at the time:

How I felt later:

What caused this to happen in the way that it did?

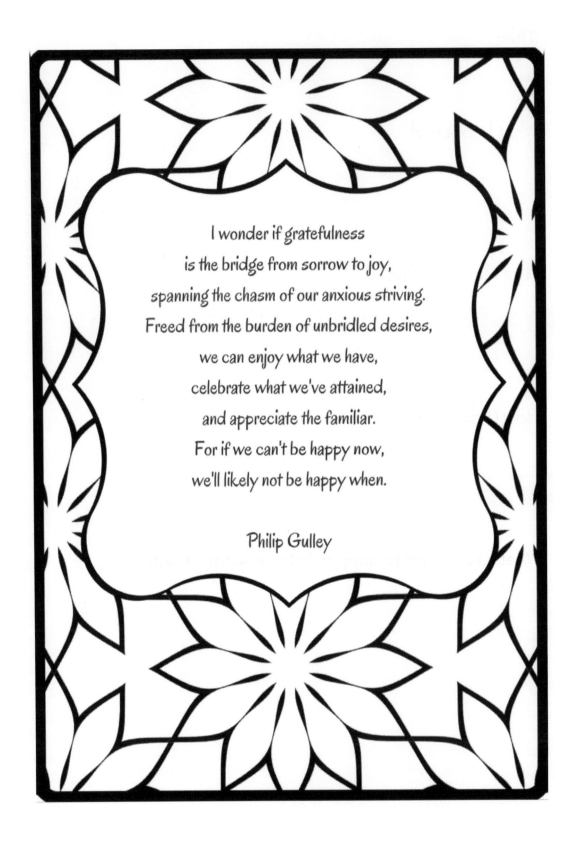

I wonder if gratefulness
is the bridge from sorrow to joy,
spanning the chasm of our anxious striving.
Freed from the burden of unbridled desires,
we can enjoy what we have,
celebrate what we've attained,
and appreciate the familiar.
For if we can't be happy now,
we'll likely not be happy when.

Philip Gulley

Today's Date:_____

Title:

What happened:

How I felt at the time:

How I felt later:

What caused this to happen in the way that it did?

When you appreciate
the good,
the good appreciates.

Tal Ben-Shahar

Today's Date:_____

Title:

What happened:

How I felt at the time:

How I felt later:

What caused this to happen in the way that it did?

When we accept ourselves
exactly as we are,
in exactly this moment,
we shift from living for tomorrow
to appreciating today.

Kris Carr

Today's Date:_____

Title:

What happened:

How I felt at the time:

How I felt later:

What caused this to happen in the way that it did?

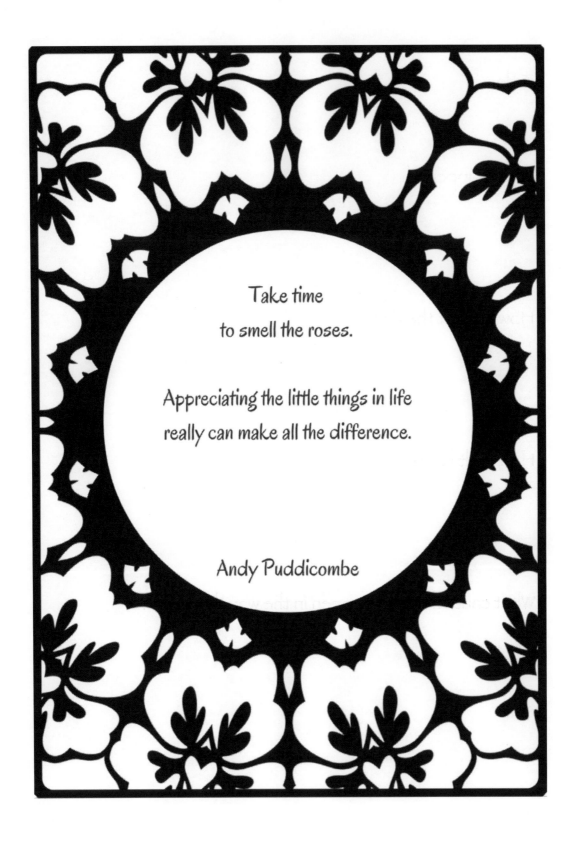

Take time
to smell the roses.

Appreciating the little things in life
really can make all the difference.

Andy Puddicombe

Today's Date:_____

Title:

What happened:

How I felt at the time:

How I felt later:

What caused this to happen in the way that it did?

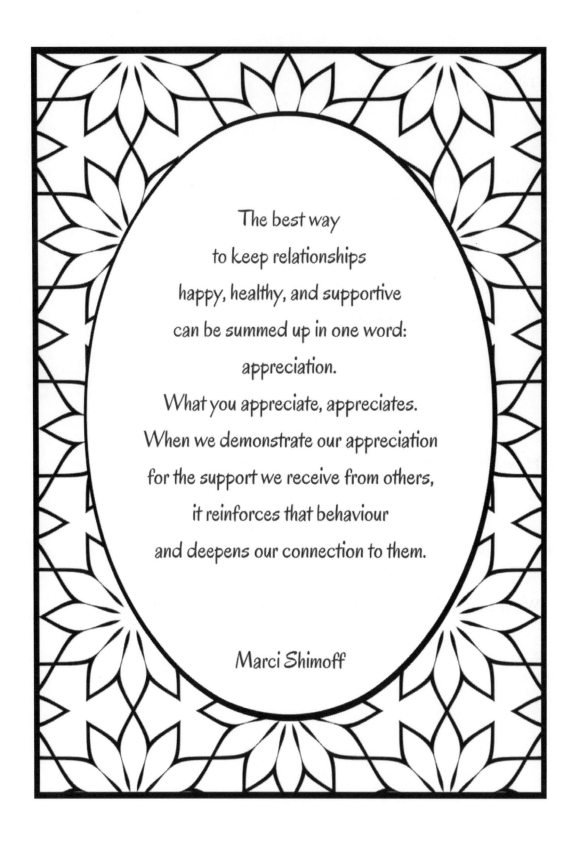

The best way
to keep relationships
happy, healthy, and supportive
can be summed up in one word:
appreciation.
What you appreciate, appreciates.
When we demonstrate our appreciation
for the support we receive from others,
it reinforces that behaviour
and deepens our connection to them.

Marci Shimoff

Title:

What happened:

How I felt at the time:

How I felt later:

What caused this to happen in the way that it did?

Three Good Things

We have reached the end of this journal, however I hope that your appreciation practice will continue for the rest of your life. What changes have you noticed in yourself, since beginning this journal? Would you like to develop your capacity for appreciation even more?

As I hope you've found, appreciation is one of the most powerful ways of creating a wholehearted life, rich with meaning, purpose and joy. Appreciation is good for us, not only mentally and emotionally, but physically too.

Many studies have found that people who frequently experience stressful emotions, such as irritation, anger, or frustration, are at significantly higher than average risk of developing cardio-vascular disease. Of course, we all feel these emotions at times, and the emotions themselves are not "bad" or "negative". Sometimes, however, they can become chronic and habitual, and this can cause problems in our relationships, our health, and our ability to enjoy life.

When we are stressed by these emotions, cortisol (stress hormone) levels increase, blood vessels constrict, blood pressure rises, and the immune system is weakened. If we experience these emotions continually, it can cause damage to the heart and other organs, and lead to serious health problems.

Developing the ability to shift out of stressful emotional reactions, to heartfelt emotions such as appreciation, love, gratitude and compassion, can have profound positive effects on our cardiovascular systems and overall health, as well as on our quality of life; most of us would prefer to experience more appreciation, love, and contentment, and less anxiety, irritation, and frustration.

Using a biofeedback device while consciously generating feelings of appreciation allows you to see when your stress levels decrease, and as you become more familiar with how that feels, you become more skilled at creating this physiological state at will. When you practise these techniques regularly, you can learn how to let go of habitual, unworkable emotional patterns, and experience more harmony and joy.

This increased awareness can improve mood, general wellbeing, and cardiovascular health. Of course, diet and exercise are essential factors in keeping the heart healthy. However, research now shows that emotional wellbeing can also play an important role in maintaining a healthy heart, especially for people recovering from heart-related illnesses.

Studies show that practising Stress Resilience techniques can help to normalise blood pressure, and increase functional capacity in patients who have suffered heart failure. This is an approach that is now used by many hospitals and cardiac rehabilitation programs.

As a Certified Stress Resilience Coach, I personally use these techniques and have seen many of my clients benefit from developing their capacity for appreciation. If you would like more information, or would like to experience the benefits of transforming stress into vitality for yourself, please visit our website:

www.darewellness.com

or connect with me on Facebook:

https://www.facebook.com/DAREWellness

Wishing you the very best!

In appreciation,

Pip Cody